GENOCIDE & PERSECUTION

Uganda

Titles in the Genocide and Persecution Series

GENOCIDE & PERSECUTION

Uganda

Myra Immell
Book Editor

Frank Chalk
Consulting Editor

GREENHAVEN PRESS
A part of Gale, Cengage Learning

GALE
CENGAGE Learning·

Detroit • New York • San Francisco • New Haven, Conn • Waterville, Maine • London

Elizabeth Des Chenes, *Director, Publishing Solutions*

© 2013 Greenhaven Press, a part of Gale, Cengage Learning

Gale and Greenhaven Press are registered trademarks used herein under license.

For more information, contact:
Greenhaven Press
27500 Drake Rd.
Farmington Hills, MI 48331-3535
Or you can visit our Internet site at gale.cengage.com.

For product information and technology assistance, contact us at:

Gale Customer Support, 1-800-877-4253
For permission to use material from this text or product, submit all requests online at www.cengage.com/permissions

Further permissions questions can be emailed to permissionrequest@cengage.com

Every effort is made to ensure that Greenhaven Press accurately reflects the original intent of the authors. Every effort has been made to trace the owners of copyrighted material.

Cover image © Chris Wayatt/Alamy.
Interior barbed wire artwork © f9photos, used under license from Shutterstock.com.

LIBRARY OF CONGRESS CATALOGING-IN-PUBLICATION DATA

Uganda / Myra Immell, book editor.
    p. cm. -- (Genocide and persecution)
    Includes bibliographical references and index.
    ISBN 978-0-7377-6258-7 (hardcover)
1. Genocide--Uganda. 2. Political violence--Uganda. 3. Crimes against humanity--Uganda. 4. Human rights--Uganda. 5. Uganda--Politics and government--20th century. I. Immell, Myra. II. Series: Genocide and persecution.
    DT433.285.U39 2012
    967.6104--dc23

                                                                2012019753

Printed in the United States of America
1 2 3 4 5 6 7 16 15 14 13 12

Contents

Chapter 1: Historical Background on Uganda

   A.B. Kasozi

   The head of Uganda's National Council for Higher Education explains
   that, since Uganda became independent in 1962, its people have endured serious violations and denial of their fundamental human and
   civil rights. Thousands of Ugandans have lost their lives, and persecution and violence have been a reality of daily life.

   The Economist

   A British magazine reports on Ugandan President Idi Amin's program
   to force all Asians out of Uganda. Although the program was amended
   and Asian citizens were not expelled, tens of thousands of Asian
   noncitizens still had to leave.

   Henry A. Kissinger

   In this 1972 memorandum to the president of the United States, a US
   government official apprises the president of the current state of affairs
   in Uganda—including Ugandan ruler Idi Amin's destruction of leaders
   of ethnic groups other than his own—and suggests what may or may
   not happen if he remains in power.

Preface

"For the dead and the living, we must
bear witness."

Elie Wiesel, Nobel laureate and
Holocaust survivor

The histories of many nations are shaped by horrific events involving torture, violent repression, and systematic mass killings. The inhumanity of such events is difficult to comprehend, yet understanding why such events take place, what impact they have on society, and how they may be prevented in the future is vitally important. The Genocide and Persecution series provides readers with anthologies of previously published materials on acts of genocide, crimes against humanity, and other instances of extreme persecution, with an emphasis on events taking place in the twentieth and twenty-first centuries. The series offers essential historical background on these significant events in modern world history, presents the issues and controversies surrounding the events, and provides first-person narratives from people whose lives were altered by the events. By providing primary sources, as well as analysis of crucial issues, these volumes help develop critical-thinking skills and support global connections. In addition, the series directly addresses curriculum standards focused on informational text and literary nonfiction and explicitly promotes literacy in history and social studies.

Each Genocide and Persecution volume focuses on genocide, crimes against humanity, or severe persecution. Material from a variety of primary and secondary sources presents a multinational perspective on the event. Articles are carefully edited and introduced to provide context for readers. The series includes volumes on significant and widely studied events like the Holocaust, as well as events that are less often studied, such as the East Pakistan genocide in what is now Bangladesh. Some volumes focus on multiple events endured by a specific people, such as the Kurds, or multiple events enacted over time by a particular oppressor or in a particular location, such as the People's Republic of China.

Each volume is organized into three chapters. The first chapter provides readers with general background information and uses primary sources such as testimony from tribunals or international courts, documents or speeches from world leaders, and legislative text. The second chapter presents multinational perspectives on issues and controversies and addresses current implications or long-lasting effects of the event. Viewpoints explore such topics as root causes; outside interventions, if any; the impact on the targeted group and the region; and the contentious issues that arose in the aftermath. The third chapter presents first-person narratives from affected people, including survivors, family members of victims, perpetrators, officials, aid workers, and other witnesses.

In addition, numerous features are included in each volume of Genocide and Persecution:

- An annotated **table of contents** provides a brief summary of each essay in the volume.

- A **foreword** gives important background information on the recognition, definition, and study of genocide in recent history and examines current efforts focused on the prevention of future atrocities.

- A **chronology** offers important dates leading up to, during, and following the event.

- **Primary sources**—including historical newspaper accounts, testimony, and personal narratives—are among the varied selections in the anthology.

- **Illustrations**—including a world map, photographs, charts, graphs, statistics, and tables—are closely tied to the text and chosen to help readers understand key points or concepts.

- **Sidebars**—including biographies of key figures and overviews of earlier or related historical events—offer additional content.

- **Pedagogical features**—including analytical exercises, writing prompts, and group activities—introduce each chapter and help reinforce the material. These features promote proficiency in writing, speaking, and listening skills and literacy in history and social studies.

- A **glossary** defines key terms, as needed.

- An annotated list of international **organizations to contact** presents sources of additional information on the volume topic.

- A **list of primary source documents** provides an annotated list of reports, treaties, resolutions, and judicial decisions related to the volume topic.

- A **for further research** section offers a bibliography of books, periodical articles, and Internet sources and an annotated section of other items such as films and websites.

- A comprehensive subject **index** provides access to key people, places, events, and subjects cited in the text.

The Genocide and Persecution series illuminates atrocities that cannot and should not be forgotten. By delving deeply into these events from a variety of perspectives, students and other readers are provided with the information they need to think critically about the past and its implications for the future.

Foreword

The term *genocide* often appears in news stories and other literature. It is not widely known, however, that the core meaning of the term comes from a legal definition, and the concept became part of international criminal law only in 1951 when the United Nations Convention on the Prevention and Punishment of the Crime of Genocide came into force. The word *genocide* appeared in print for the first time in 1944 when Raphael Lemkin, a Polish Jewish refugee from Adolf Hitler's World War II invasion of Eastern Europe, invented the term and explored its meaning in his pioneering book *Axis Rule in Occupied Europe.*

Humanity's Recognition of Genocide and Persecution

Lemkin understood that throughout the history of the human race there have always been leaders who thought they could solve their problems not only through victory in war, but also by destroying entire national, ethnic, racial, or religious groups. Such annihilations of entire groups, in Lemkin's view, deprive the world of the very cultural diversity and richness in languages, traditions, values, and practices that distinguish the human race from all other life on earth. Genocide is not only unjust, it threatens the very existence and progress of human civilization, in Lemkin's eyes.

Looking to the past, Lemkin understood that the prevailing coarseness and brutality of earlier human societies and the lower value placed on human life obscured the existence of genocide. Sacrifice and exploitation, as well as torture and public execution, had been common at different times in history. Looking toward a more humane future, Lemkin asserted the need to punish— and when possible prevent—a crime for which there had been no name until he invented it.

Legal Definitions of Genocide

On December 9, 1948, the United Nations adopted its Convention on the Prevention and Punishment of the Crime of Genocide (UNGC). Under Article II, genocide

> means any of the following acts committed with intent to destroy, in whole or in part, a national, ethnical, racial or religious group, as such:
>
> (a) Killing members of the group;
>
> (b) Causing serious bodily or mental harm to members of the group;
>
> (c) Deliberately inflicting on the group conditions of life calculated to bring about its physical destruction in whole or in part;
>
> (d) Imposing measures intended to prevent births within the group;
>
> (e) Forcibly transferring children of the group to another group.

Article III of the convention defines the elements of the crime of genocide, making punishable:

> (a) Genocide;
>
> (b) Conspiracy to commit genocide;
>
> (c) Direct and public incitement to commit genocide;
>
> (d) Attempt to commit genocide;
>
> (e) Complicity in genocide.

After intense debate, the architects of the convention excluded acts committed with intent to destroy social, political, and economic groups from the definition of genocide. Thus, attempts to destroy whole social classes—the physically and mentally challenged, and homosexuals, for example—are not acts of genocide under the terms of the UNGC. These groups achieved a belated but very significant measure of protection under international criminal law in the Rome Statute of the International Criminal

Court, adopted at a conference on July 17, 1998, and entered into force on July 1, 2002.

The Rome Statute defined a crime against humanity in the following way:

> any of the following acts when committed as part of a wide-spread and systematic attack directed against any civilian population:
>
> (a) Murder;
>
> (b) Extermination;
>
> (c) Enslavement;
>
> (d) Deportation or forcible transfer of population;
>
> (e) Imprisonment or other severe deprivation of physical liberty in violation of fundamental rules of international law;
>
> (f) Torture;
>
> (g) Rape, sexual slavery, enforced prostitution, forced pregnancy, enforced sterilization, or any other form of sexual violence of comparable gravity;
>
> (h) Persecution against any identifiable group or collectivity on political, racial, national, ethnic, cultural, religious, gender . . . or other grounds that are universally recognized as impermissible under international law, in connection with any act referred to in this paragraph or any crime within the jurisdiction of this Court;
>
> (i) Enforced disappearance of persons;
>
> (j) The crime of apartheid;
>
> (k) Other inhumane acts of a similar character intentionally causing great suffering, or serious injury to body or to mental or physical health.

Although genocide is often ranked as "the crime of crimes," in practice prosecutors find it much easier to convict perpetrators of crimes against humanity rather than genocide under domestic laws. However, while Article I of the UNGC declares that countries adhering to the UNGC recognize genocide as "a crime under international law which they undertake to prevent and to punish," the Rome Statute provides no comparable international mechanism for the prosecution of crimes against humanity. A treaty would help individual countries and international institutions introduce measures to prevent crimes against humanity, as well as open more avenues to the domestic and international prosecution of war criminals.

The Evolving Laws of Genocide

In the aftermath of the serious crimes committed against civilians in the former Yugoslavia since 1991 and the Rwanda genocide of 1994, the United Nations Security Council created special international courts to bring the alleged perpetrators of these events to justice. While the UNGC stands as the standard definition of genocide in law, the new courts contributed significantly to today's nuanced meaning of genocide, crimes against humanity, ethnic cleansing, and serious war crimes in international criminal law.

Also helping to shape contemporary interpretations of such mass atrocity crimes are the special and mixed courts for Sierra Leone, Cambodia, Lebanon, and Iraq, which may be the last of their type in light of the creation of the International Criminal Court (ICC), with its broad jurisdiction over mass atrocity crimes in all countries that adhere to the Rome Statute of the ICC. The Yugoslavia and Rwanda tribunals have already clarified the law of genocide, ruling that rape can be prosecuted as a weapon in committing genocide, evidence of intent can be absent when convicting low-level perpetrators of genocide, and public incitement to commit genocide is a crime even if genocide does not immediately follow the incitement.

Several current controversies about genocide are worth noting and will require more research in the future:

1. Dictators accused of committing genocide or persecution may hold onto power more tightly for fear of becoming

vulnerable to prosecution after they step down. Therefore, do threats of international indictments of these alleged perpetrators actually delay transfers of power to more representative rulers, thereby causing needless suffering?

2. Would the large sum of money spent for international retributive justice be better spent on projects directly benefiting the survivors of genocide and persecution?

3. Can international courts render justice impartially or do they deliver only "victors' justice," that is the application of one set of rules to judge the vanquished and a different and laxer set of rules to judge the victors?

It is important to recognize that the law of genocide is constantly evolving, and scholars searching for the roots and early warning signs of genocide may prefer to use their own definitions of genocide in their work. While the UNGC stands as the standard definition of genocide in law, the debate over its interpretation and application will never end. The ultimate measure of the value of any definition of genocide is its utility for identifying the roots of genocide and preventing future genocides.

Motives for Genocide and Early Warning Signs

When identifying past cases of genocide, many scholars work with some version of the typology of motives published in 1990 by historian Frank Chalk and sociologist Kurt Jonassohn in their book *The History and Sociology of Genocide*. The authors identify the following four motives and acknowledge that they may overlap, or several lesser motives might also drive a perpetrator:

1. To eliminate a real or potential threat, as in Imperial Rome's decision to annihilate Carthage in 146 BC.

2. To spread terror among real or potential enemies, as in Genghis Khan's destruction of city-states and people who rebelled against the Mongols in the thirteenth century.

3. To acquire economic wealth, as in the case of the Massachusetts Puritans' annihilation of the native Pequot people in 1637.
4. To implement a belief, theory, or an ideology, as in the case of Germany's decision under Hitler and the Nazis to destroy completely the Jewish people of Europe from 1941 to 1945.

Although these motives represent differing goals, they share common early warning signs of genocide. A good example of genocide in recent times that could have been prevented through close attention to early warning signs was the genocide of 1994 inflicted on the people labeled as "Tutsi" in Rwanda. Between 1959 and 1963, the predominantly Hutu political parties in power stigmatized all Tutsi as members of a hostile racial group, violently forcing their leaders and many civilians into exile in neighboring countries through a series of assassinations and massacres. Despite systematic exclusion of Tutsi from service in the military, government security agencies, and public service, as well as systematic discrimination against them in higher education, hundreds of thousands of Tutsi did remain behind in Rwanda. Government-issued cards identified each Rwandan as Hutu or Tutsi.

A generation later, some Tutsi raised in refugee camps in Uganda and elsewhere joined together, first organizing politically and then militarily, to reclaim a place in their homeland. When the predominantly Tutsi Rwanda Patriotic Front invaded Rwanda from Uganda in October 1990, extremist Hutu political parties demonized all of Rwanda's Tutsi as traitors, ratcheting up hate propaganda through radio broadcasts on government-run Radio Rwanda and privately owned radio station RTLM. Within the print media, *Kangura* and other publications used vicious cartoons to further demonize Tutsi and to stigmatize any Hutu who dared advocate bringing Tutsi into the government. Massacres of dozens and later hundreds of Tutsi sprang up even as Rwandans prepared to elect a coalition government led by moderate political parties, and as the United Nations dispatched a small international military force led by Canadian general Roméo Dallaire to oversee the elections and political transition. Late in 1992, an international human rights organization's investigating team detected the hate propaganda campaign, verified systematic massacres of Tutsi, and warned the international community that Rwanda had already entered the early stages of genocide, to no avail. On April 6, 1994, Rwanda's genocidal killing accelerated at an alarming pace when someone shot down the airplane flying Rwandan president Juvenal Habyarimana home from peace talks in Arusha, Tanzania.

Hundreds of thousands of Tutsi civilians—including children, women, and the elderly—died horrible deaths because the world ignored the early warning signs of the genocide and refused to act. Prominent among those early warning signs were: 1) systematic, government-decreed discrimination against the Tutsi as members of a supposed racial group; 2) government-issued identity cards labeling every Tutsi as a member of a racial group; 3) hate propaganda casting all Tutsi as subversives and traitors; 4) organized assassinations and massacres targeting Tutsi; and 5) indoctrination of militias and special military units to believe that all Tutsi posed a genocidal threat to the existence of Hutu and would enslave Hutu if they ever again became the rulers of Rwanda.

Genocide Prevention and the Responsibility to Protect

The shock waves emanating from the Rwanda genocide forced world leaders at least to acknowledge in principle that the national sovereignty of offending nations cannot trump the responsibility of those governments to prevent the infliction of mass atrocities on their own people. When governments violate that obligation, the member states of the United Nations have a responsibility to get involved. Such involvement can take the form of, first, offering to help the local government change its ways through technical advice and development aid, and second—if the local government persists in assaulting its own people—initiating armed intervention to protect the civilians at risk. In 2005 the United Nations began to implement the Responsibility to Protect initiative, a framework of principles to guide the international community in preventing mass atrocities.

As in many real-world domains, theory and practice often diverge. Genocide and crimes against humanity are rooted in problems that produce failing states: poverty, poor education, extreme nationalism, lawlessness, dictatorship, and corruption. Implementing the principles of the Responsibility to Protect doctrine burdens intervening state leaders with the necessity of addressing each of those problems over a long period of time. And when those problems prove too intractable and complex to solve easily, the citizens of the intervening nations may lose patience, voting out the leader who initiated the intervention. Arguments based solely on humanitarian principles fail to overcome such concerns. What is needed to persuade political leaders to stop preventable mass atrocities are compelling arguments based on their own national interests.

Preventable mass atrocities threaten the national interests of all states in five specific ways:

1. Mass atrocities create conditions that engender widespread and concrete threats from terrorism, piracy, and other forms of lawlessness on the land and sea;

2. Mass atrocities facilitate the spread of warlordism, whose tentacles block affordable access to vital raw materials produced in the affected country and threaten the prosperity of all nations that depend on the consumption of these resources;

3. Mass atrocities trigger cascades of refugees and internally displaced populations that, combined with climate change and growing international air travel, will accelerate the worldwide incidence of lethal infectious diseases;

4. Mass atrocities spawn single-interest parties and political agendas that drown out more diverse political discourse in the countries where the atrocities take place and in the countries that host large numbers of refugees. Xenophobia and nationalist backlashes are the predictable consequences of government indifference to mass atrocities elsewhere that could have been prevented through early actions;

5. Mass atrocities foster the spread of national and transnational criminal networks trafficking in drugs, women, arms, contraband, and laundered money.

Alerting elected political representatives to the consequences of mass atrocities should be part of every student movement's agenda in the twenty-first century. Adam Smith, the great political economist and author of *The Wealth of Nations*, put it best when he wrote: "It is not from the benevolence of the butcher, the brewer, or the baker that we expect our dinner, but from their regard to their own interest." Self-interest is a powerful engine for good in the marketplace and can be an equally powerful motive and source of inspiration for state action to prevent genocide and mass persecution. In today's new global village, the lives we save may be our own.

Frank Chalk

Frank Chalk, who has a doctorate from the University of Wisconsin-Madison, is a professor of history and director of the Montreal Institute for Genocide and Human Rights Studies at Concordia University in Montreal, Canada. He is coauthor, with Kurt

Jonassohn, of The History and Sociology of Genocide *(1990); coauthor with General Roméo Dallaire, Kyle Matthews, Carla Barqueiro, and Simon Doyle of* Mobilizing the Will to Intervene: Leadership to Prevent Mass Atrocities *(2010); and associate editor of the three-volume Macmillan Reference USA* Encyclopedia of Genocide and Crimes Against Humanity *(2004). Chalk served as president of the International Association of Genocide Scholars from June 1999 to June 2001. His current research focuses on the use of radio and television broadcasting in the incitement and prevention of genocide, and domestic laws on genocide. For more information on genocide and examples of the experiences of people displaced by genocide and other human rights violations, interested readers can consult the websites of the Montreal Institute for Genocide and Human Rights Studies (http://migs.concordia.ca) and the Montreal Life Stories project (www.lifestoriesmontreal.ca).*

World Map

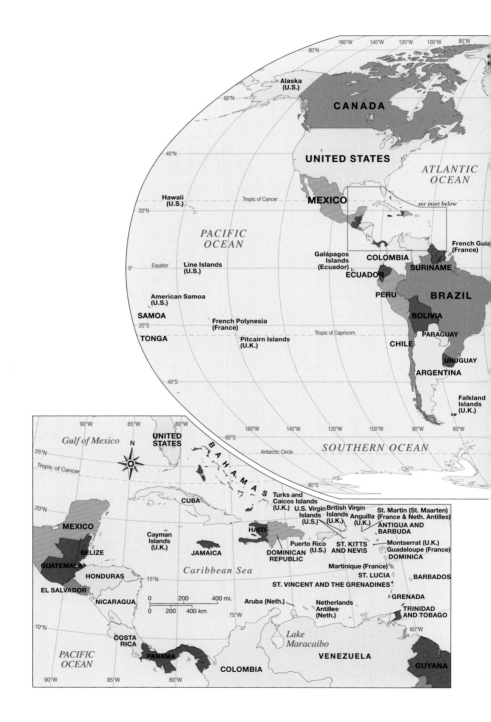

160°W 140°W 120°W 100°W 80°W

80°N

Alaska
(U.S.)

60°N

CANADA

40°N

UNITED STATES

ATLANTIC
OCEAN

Hawaii
(U.S.)

Tropic of Cancer

MEXICO

see inset below

20°N

PACIFIC
OCEAN

French Guia
(France)

Galápagos
Islands
(Ecuador)

COLOMBIA

Line Islands
(U.S.)

SURINAME

Equator

0°

ECUADOR

American Samoa
(U.S.)

PERU

BRAZIL

SAMOA

20°S

French Polynesia
(France)

BOLIVIA

Tropic of Capricorn

PARAGUAY

TONGA

Pitcairn Islands
(U.K.)

CHILE

URUGUAY

ARGENTINA

40°S

Falkland
Islands
(U.K.)

90°W 85°W 80°W

160°W 140°W 120°W 100°W 80°W 60°W

60°S

Gulf of Mexico

N

UNITED
STATES

Antarctic Circle

SOUTHERN OCEAN

25°N

Tropic of Cancer

80°S

Turks and
Caicos Islands
(U.K.)

CUBA

20°N

U.S. Virgin British Virgin
Islands Islands
(U.S.) (U.K.)

St. Martin (St. Maarten)
Anguilla (France & Neth. Antilles)
(U.K.)

MEXICO

Cayman
Islands
(U.K.)

HAITI

ANTIGUA AND
BARBUDA

BELIZE

JAMAICA

Puerto Rico
(U.S.)

DOMINICAN
REPUBLIC

ST. KITTS
AND NEVIS

Montserrat (U.K.)
Guadeloupe (France)

DOMINICA

GUATEMALA

HONDURAS

15°N

Caribbean Sea

Martinique (France)

ST. LUCIA

BARBADOS

ST. VINCENT AND THE GRENADINES

EL SALVADOR

NICARAGUA

0 200 400 mi.

0 200 400 km

75°W

Aruba (Neth.)

Netherlands
Antilles
(Neth.)

GRENADA

TRINIDAD
AND TOBAGO

10°N

COSTA
RICA

60°W

PACIFIC
OCEAN

PANAMA

Lake
Maracaibo

VENEZUELA

GUYANA

90°W 85°W 80°W

COLOMBIA

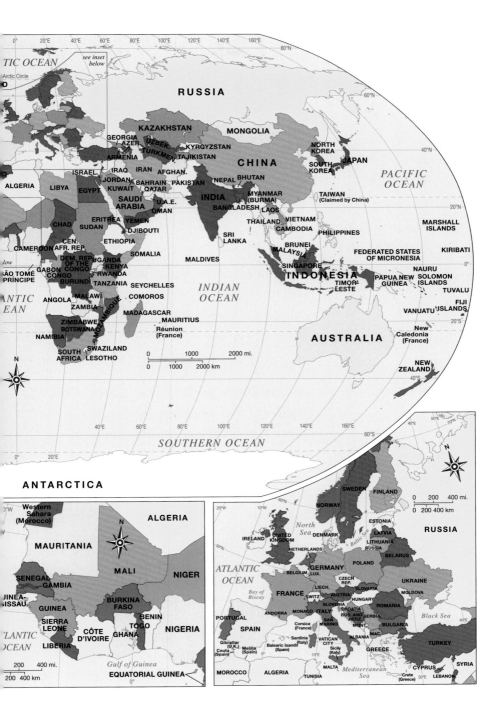

Chronology

1894	Uganda becomes a British protectorate.
1958	Uganda is given internal self-government.
1960	The Uganda People's Congress, a political party that draws its support from the northern regions of the country, is formed with Milton Obote as its president.
1962	Uganda gains independence from Britain; Milton Obote becomes prime minister; Uganda is admitted as a member state to the United Nations.
1963	Uganda becomes a republic.
1966	Milton Obote abolishes the offices of the president and vice president, appoints himself president and commander-in-chief of the armed forces, announces the suspension of the constitution, and ends autonomy in subnational kingdom Burganda.
1967	A new constitution comes into effect, making Uganda a republic and vesting considerable power in the president.
1971	General Idi Amin stages a successful military coup to overthrow Milton Obote's government and declares himself president of Uganda; Amin begins a reign of terror during which brutality

and corruption are rampant, ethnic minorities are persecuted, and hundreds of thousands of Ugandans are killed.

1972   Idi Amin orders the expulsion of thousands of Asian workers and business people and confiscates their businesses and assets for himself and his supporters; Ugandan exiles who oppose Amin's government invade Uganda from Tanzania.

1973   Many well-known Ugandans start to go missing.

1974   Idi Amin establishes the Commission of Inquiry into the Disappearances of People in Uganda to investigate disappearances between January 25, 1971 and the time of the commission in 1974.

1976   Idi Amin declares himself president of Uganda for life; Britain breaks off diplomatic relations with Uganda; violence escalates throughout the country.

1979   Many religious groups are banned from operating in Uganda; a coalition of Tanzanian troops and Ugandan exiles attack Uganda and oust Amin.

1980   Milton Obote returns from exile and is elected president in a disputed election.

1981   Yoweri Museveni forms an anti-Obote guerrilla group that becomes known as the National Resistance Army (NRA); the NRA begins a five-year bush war against the Obote government that

	claims hundreds of thousands of lives and causes thousands of Ugandans to seek refuge in neighboring countries.
1983	Milton Obote's National Liberation Army, many members of which are Acholi, forces out almost the entire West Nile district, Idi Amin's home region, to retaliate for the abuses they had endured when Amin was in power.
1983–1984	Thousands of civilians are massacred in the Luwero Triangle by Milton Obote's government troops.
1985	Alice Auna forms the Holy Spirit Movement and takes the name Alice Lakwena; Milton Obote is overthrown in a military coup by factions within his own army, the National Liberation Army; Joseph Kony becomes spiritual advisor to northern rebels and eventually forms his own militia, the Uganda People's Democratic Christian Army.
1986	The NRA takes power; Yoweri Museveni proclaims a government of national unity, with himself as president; Alice Lakwena converts her followers into the Holy Spirit Mobile Forces and rebels against the government.
1987	Alice Lakwena's Holy Spirit Movement army is defeated and she flees to Kenya; Joseph Kony and his rebel group wage war against the Ugandan government and a vicious campaign against the

Acholi in northern Uganda—massacring and maiming civilians, looting villages, abducting children, and forcing abducted children to serve as soldiers, porters, or sex slaves.

1988   Joseph Kony becomes the sole rebel leader in northern Uganda.

1991   Joseph Kony changes the name of his rebel group from Uganda People's Democratic Christian Army to the Lord's Resistance Army (LRA).

1994   Peace talks between the government and the LRA fail.

1995   Uganda adopts a new constitution but maintains a ban on political activity.

1996   Museveni wins Uganda's first presidential election in sixteen years by a landslide.

2001   Museveni wins another presidential election.

2002   Sudan agrees to permit the Ugandan army to cross into South Sudan to attack Kony's bases; the army evacuates more than four hundred thousand civilians caught up in the fight against the LRA.

2002–2004   Kony launches vicious counterattacks in northern Uganda and southern Sudan, and the war intensifies across the north.

2003   Idi Amin dies in Saudi Arabia; President Museveni asks the International Criminal Court (ICC) to investigate war

	crimes and crimes against humanity committed by the LRA.
2004	LRA rebels slaughter more than two hundred displaced people in northern Uganda; the Ugandan government and the LRA hold their first face-to-face peace talks.
2005	Milton Obote dies in Johannesburg, South Africa; presidential term limits are abolished; the International Criminal Court issues arrest warrants for the five LRA commanders, including Kony.
2006	The LRA declares a cease-fire, leaves Uganda, and signs a truce with the Ugandan government; peace talks begin in Juba, South Sudan, between Uganda and the LRA; Museveni wins a disputed presidential election.
2008	A peace agreement is reached between the LRA and Uganda; Kony refuses to sign the peace agreement.
2009	Ugandan soldiers clash with the LRA; Ugandan Parliament member David Bahati proposes a controversial Anti-Homosexuality Bill to Parliament.
2010	A Ugandan newspaper, the *Rolling Stone,* publishes names and pictures of men identified as gay.
2011	Museveni wins another presidential election.

Historical Background on Uganda

Chapter Exercises

STATISTICS	Uganda
Total Area	241,038 sq km; World ranking: 81
Population	34,612,250; World ranking: 36
Ethnic Groups	Baganda 16.9%, Banyakole 9.5%, Basoga 8.4%, Bakiga 6.9%, Iteso 6.4%, Langi 6.1%, Acholi 4.7%, Bagisu 4.6%, Lugbara 4.2%, Bunyoro 2.7%, other 29.6%
Languages	English, Ganda, Luganda, other Niger-Congo languages, Nilo-Saharan languages, Swahili, Arabic
Religions	Roman Catholic 41.9%, Protestant 42% (Anglican 35.9%, Pentecostal 4.6%, Seventh-Day Adventist 1.5%), Muslim 12.1%, other 3.1%, none 0.9%
Literacy (total population)	66.8%
GDP	$42.15 billion; World ranking: 97
Labor Force (by occupation)	Agriculture 82%, Industry 5%, Services 13%

Source: *The World Factbook*. Washington, DC: Central Intelligence Agency, 2012. www.cia.gov.

1. Analyzing Statistics

Question 1: Examine the statistics regarding ethnic groups in Uganda. Which group or groups are primarily responsible for the human rights violations in Uganda? Which group has been the major target of persecution? Given the statistics, are these the groups you would expect to be the perpetrators and the victims? Why or why not?

Question 2: The statistics regarding religion show that Protestants and Catholics far outnumber other religious groups in Uganda. Do you think religion played a major role in the human rights violations in Uganda or were other factors more important?

Question 3: Examine the statistics regarding Uganda's labor force. What do the statistics tell you about the importance of agriculture to the nation and to the people? What effect do you think the human rights abuses in northern Uganda have had on people's livelihoods, the nation's ability to export product, and the GDP?

2. Writing Prompt

Write a newspaper article describing the human rights situation in Uganda under President Milton Obote. Include a catchy headline for the article, personal information about Obote that helps explain the human rights violations during his regimes, and the role of the army in perpetuating terror among Ugandans.

3. Group Activity

In small groups examine Idi Amin's human rights abuses. Then write and present a speech recommending actions the international community should take against Amin and his regime.

Genocide and Persecution in Uganda: An Overview

A.B. Kasozi

In the following viewpoint, Ugandan researcher A.B. Kasozi provides an overview of violations of human and civil rights in Uganda since 1962. Millions of people have been massacred, maimed, thrown into prison (often without trial), forced to leave the country, or denied other fundamental human rights. Certain ethnic groups have been targeted for genocide, Kasozi explains, and government-sponsored violence has been rampant. Civil rights, such as freedom of opinion and right of association, have been denied as well. During certain periods, the state has controlled the media; political parties, trade unions, student organizations, and some religious organizations were condemned, forbidden, or banned. Kasozi is head of Uganda's National Council for Higher Education. He has authored a number of books on Uganda, including The Social Origins of Violence in Uganda, 1964–1985.

Since 1962, Ugandans have suffered gross violation of human rights, including genocide, government-sponsored violence, acts of elimination of elites, forced exiles and expulsions, imprisonment without trial, and denial of the other basic human rights.

A.B. Kasozi, "Uganda," *Encyclopedia of Genocide and Crimes Against Humanity*. New York: Macmillan Reference USA, 2005, pp. 1053–1055. Copyright © 2005 by Cengage Learning. All rights reserved. Reproduced by permission.

More than 2 million people have been killed, maimed, imprisoned, or forced into exile. Various political elites have sought power to control and to distribute resources at the expense of human rights. Ugandans have not yet developed mechanisms to change government leaders by peaceful means. Political change has been effected through violence, and this has invariably led to other forms of violence. The distribution of resources along ethnic and racial lines was a legacy of British colonialism. During the colonial period, the Europeans and Asians received the highest incomes because they controlled the state and business, respectively. Among the African population, the Baganda were the richest because they produced cash crops—cotton and coffee—and played the role of colonial subimperialists. Western Uganda became a reservoir of labor for the colonial state as well as the managers of the cash crop economy in Buganda. The armed forces of the colonial era were recruited mainly from the Luo and Sudanic speakers of the northern region. This specialization along racial and ethnic lines became the source of instability and violence in postcolonial Uganda. Unsophisticated leaders like [Milton] Obote and [Idi] Amin exploited the politics of ethnicity and historical imbalances to entrench themselves. They branded whole populations guilty for the inequities of British colonialism and imposed collective punishment regardless of class or political association and sympathies.

Thousands of Ugandans have suffered from acts of genocidal massacre. Since independence in 1962, Uganda has witnessed massacres directed against certain ethnic and consolidated social groups. Between 1966 and 1971, the first Obote regime targeted the Baganda, and 400 to 1,000 people were reported to have been killed. The Amin Regime (1971–1979) targeted the Acholi and Langi, particularly those in the armed forces, and thousands were eliminated. During the Tanzania-led war to oust Amin, groups of people suspected of supporting or sympathizing with Amin or even those who only came from the ethnic groups in his home region were killed. These included Muslims in the Ankole-

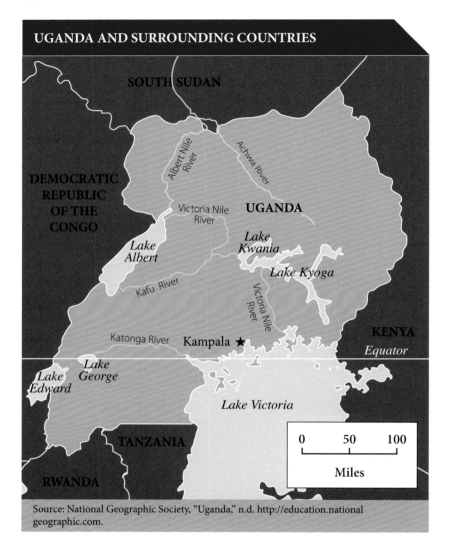

UGANDA AND SURROUNDING COUNTRIES

SOUTH SUDAN

DEMOCRATIC REPUBLIC OF THE CONGO

Albert Nile River

Achwa River

Victoria Nile River

UGANDA

Lake Albert

Lake Kwania

Lake Kyoga

Kafu River

Victoria Nile River

Katonga River

Kampala ★

KENYA

Equator

Lake Edward

Lake George

Lake Victoria

TANZANIA

RWANDA

0   50   100

Miles

Source: National Geographic Society, "Uganda," n.d. http://education.national
geographic.com.

Masaka areas, the people of West Nile, and Nubians scattered in the urban centers. In the second Obote administration (1980– 1985), the Baganda were again targets for killings. The activities of both the government and the guerrilla armies in the Luwero Triangle caused the deaths of more than 300,000 people and the flight of many more from the area. From 1986 to 2003, the people of the Acholi region in northern Uganda were indiscriminately terrorized. More than 100,000 people were killed and more than 20,000 children abducted. These killings were managed by individuals trying to destabilize the political machinery of the Uganda state.

Elimination of Elites, Exiles and Expulsions, and Denial of Basic Human Rights

The violent struggle to control the state has led those in power to eliminate their political rivals. In the period from 1962 to 1971, many political opponents of the first Obote regime were either imprisoned . . . or forced into exile. When Amin came to power, he eliminated political and commercial elites who seemed to be a threat to his grip on Uganda. Those killed in the Amin period . . . included prominent individuals such as Chief Justice Ben Kiwanuka, the Anglican Archbishop Janan Luwum, writers such as Byron Kawaddwa, Father Clement Kiggundu, and prominent business people. The elimination of prominent individuals continued throughout the Uganda National Liberation Front (UNLF) governments (1979–1980), the second Obote administration (1980–1985), the Okello junta years (1985–1986), and the early part of the National Resistance Movement (NRM) government. The impact of these eliminations has been the reduction of the number of individuals capable of offering alternative leadership to [Uganda].

Since 1969, Uganda has lost thousands of people through exile and expulsions. During the Amin regime, more than 80,000 people were forced to leave Uganda. By 1984, about a quarter of a million Ugandans were living in exile as refugees. In the period from 1980 to 1983, almost the whole of the West Nile district population was forced into exile by the atrocities committed by the Uganda National Liberation Army.

Whole ethnic and social groups have been expelled from Uganda. In October and November 1969, Obote's government expelled about 30,000 Kenyan workers, most of them Luos. Their brutal expulsion did not make headlines in the international news because no strong international economic interests were involved. In 1972, Idi Amin expelled some 75,000 Asians of Indo-Pakistani origin and appropriated their properties. Although they have been compensated and some have returned, the action was a brutal one. In 1982–1983, functionaries of the official ruling party, the Uganda People's Congress (UPC), caused the expulsion of some 75,000 Banyarwanda who had over the years settled in western Uganda. . . . In the same period, the UPC government fanned primordial forces within Karamoja that led to internal conflicts in that region. Some 20,000 to 40,000 Karamajog were killed, and many were displaced in the same period.

Between 1966 and 1986, Ugandans were denied basic human rights. The right to freedom of opinion was denied, as was the right of association. The media was state controlled, and political parties, trade unions, student organizations, and later, some religious organizations were proscribed. There was, particularly in the period after 1971 to 1985, complete absence of the rule of law. Court verdicts were not respected by the security forces. The security forces could arrest people without warrant and detain them for as long as they wished. But these forces were immune from prosecution. When the [Yoweri] Museveni government came to power in 1986, it instituted a commission of inquiry into past human rights abuses and the creation of the Human Rights Commission. The situation dramatically changed for the better.

The 1995 Constitution

The 1995 Constitution put in place mechanisms facilitating conflict resolution, including separation of powers among the executive, legislative, and judicial branches of government. However, permanent peace and security can only be viable when Ugandans accept, in word and deed, the mechanisms for changing the guard without violence as embedded in the 1995 Constitution.

The Expulsion of Uganda's Asian Population

The Economist

In the following viewpoint, The Economist provides insight on Ugandan president Idi Amin's 1972 dictate that Asians must leave Uganda. Amin's original plan was to expel all Asians. He quickly replaced it with one that expelled noncitizen Asians only, most likely because he realized that he would be accused of racism if he expelled Asian citizens. The author explains that all those leaving had to relinquish their businesses and other property to the government for sale to African buyers. Asians claiming to be citizens had to verify their citizenship. Those who did not prove citizenship to the government's satisfaction had to leave after the noncitizen emigration was accomplished. The Economist asserts that limiting the expulsion to noncitizen Asians reduced the human and economic problems that would have resulted from an expulsion of all Asians, but even for those Asian Ugandans allowed to stay, their status in Uganda was precarious.

In circumstances that seemed to rule out any hint of flexibility, President [Idi] Amin decided on Tuesday [August 22, 1972] to drop the plan he had announced three days earlier to expel all

The Expulsion of Ugandan Asians: Recommendations from Thomas Melady, US Ambassador to Uganda

1. We recommend that the USG [United States government] maintain a strict policy of no public comment in regard to the Asian expulsion [activities] of General [Idi] Amin.

2. In this very moving human tragedy it is practically guaranteed that there will be additional events that, like the primary act itself, will be in violation of human rights. Any action by the USG in commenting or taking the leadership in statements and/or activities condemning these activities would be mis-interpreted as an act of intervention in the internal affairs of Uganda. Our relations for the moment are fragile and such an action would certainly complicate them. Furthermore any such action would [be] counterproductive.

3. Let us hope that African leaders who do not hesitate to take advantage of every opportunity to attack South Africa and Rhodesia for their violation of human rights and who also at-tack the US and UK [United Kingdom] for alleged violations of human rights will have the courage to take the leadership in any UN [United Nations] or international effort to end the

of Uganda's Asian citizens. Why this change of heart? Certainly not just because Mr Julius Nyerere, [president] in neighbouring Tanzania, had criticised him. Nor because of opposition from Ugandan university students, who discreetly reminded him that all Ugandan citizens were his government's responsibility.

The real deciding factor seems to have been President Amin's own realisation that any such blanket expulsion of Asians would leave him with no defence against charges of racialism. In this Mr Nyerere's strictures may have played their part, but the main im-pulse probably came from Uganda's foreign minister, Mr Wanume violation of the human rights of Asians of various nationalities living in Uganda. President Nyerere [of Tanzania] has already spoken, a prominent African church group and several east African newspapers have criticized some aspects of Amin's expulsion order. Perhaps others will follow and take the matter to the UN. . . .

4. One way for us to help Asians—if a decision is taken to do this—would be to find an Arab leader who . . . could approach Amin. I do not recommend that we do this. We are cultivating our embassy contacts with the Sudanese and Libyans for future use when the need arises. We want to preserve whatever credits we have to serve more concrete bilateral concerns.

5. I feel best efforts we could make on humanitarian side, without ill effect to our bilateral relations, would be . . . to offer special immigration to small group of expellees who will be, for all practical purposes, stateless. I can assure you that this gesture—however nominal—would be well received by the British and Indian high commissions in Kampala [Uganda] and I would believe also by their governments.

US Department of State Office of the Historian,
Document from Foreign Relations of the United
States, 1969–1976, vol. E-5, Part 1, Documents on
Sub-Saharan Africa. http://history.state.gov.

Kibedi, who was in Europe at the time of his president's first announcement. Mr Kibedi's defence of the expulsion programme was based throughout on the argument that citizenship and not race was the criterion for departure. It was not a good defence, since it did not take into account all the non-citizen Europeans who would still remain in Uganda, but it was better than nothing.

A Required Exodus for Asian Non-Citizens

The decision to allow Uganda's Asian citizens to stay on does not affect the 60,000 Asian non-citizens here, who still have to leave by early November. The first 12,000 to 15,000 departing British Asians will be flown to Britain next month, so that by the time [British government official] Mr Geoffrey Rippon arrives in [the Ugandan capital of] Kampala for his second visit early in October he will have sufficient proof of Britain's good faith to persuade President Amin (or so the British Government hopes) to extend the November 7th time limit for the remainder to get out. By then there should be about 40,000 non-citizen Asians left, 25,000 of them wanting to go to Britain, the remainder British and Indian Asians who plan to settle in India.

Last week President Amin decreed that all businesses, buildings and industries owned by non-citizen Asians here must be registered with the authorities by the end of this month. But the registration forms are still being printed. So are the application forms that prospective African buyers of businesses relinquished by Asians have been invited to fill in. Mr Amin has said that all property belonging to departing Asians, except personal effects, must be disposed of by the government, and not by private sale or by transfer to (presumably African or European) relatives. In this context prospective African buyers have been told that they may expect government assistance—but where the resources for this will come from, or the foreign exchange to remit payments to the Asian sellers overseas, has nowhere been stated. It has not even been decided how much money Asian emigrants will be allowed to take with them, and what will happen to the remainder of their capital here after they go. Until at least some of these points receive attention, the exodus will be delayed.

A Quantitative Rather than a Qualitative Move

Mr Amin's decision to limit the expulsion programme to non-citizen Asians has certainly reduced the immediate human and economic problems. The wealthiest Ugandan Asians will now remain. The government will not be faced with the task of buying up in the space of a few months large enterprises like the Madhvani industrial group, the value of which roughly equals a quarter of Uganda's annual budget. Nor will there be a total disruption of the social services: some Asian doctors will stay; so will numbers of mechanics, engineers and technicians.

But the president's retraction is a quantitative rather than a qualitative move. Of the 23,000 Asians here who claim Ugandan citizenship, about half are expected to lose it during the current verification campaign. The British high commissioner, Mr Richard Slater, has hinted that a few of these people may be allowed to settle in Britain. The rest will become stateless and, under the terms of Mr Amin's decision, they will have to leave Uganda after the non-citizen exodus is completed.

For the 10,000 or so who should qualify as accepted Ugandan citizens, there is still the problem of what comes next. Justifying his initial decision to expel Asian Ugandan citizens as well as the rest, Mr Amin spoke of "acts of arson and sabotage" that the Asian community was perpetrating or planning to start. He has said that Asian citizens have collaborated with their non-citizen fellows, and that he awaits the day when there will be no Asians in Uganda. His tactics may change, but his objective will remain the same.

Idi Amin Is a Repressive Ruler

Henry A. Kissinger

In the following viewpoint, presidential adviser Henry A. Kissinger offers an appraisal of the situation in Uganda in a 1972 memorandum to US president Richard Nixon. He explains that Ugandan president Idi Amin has shown himself to be determined to wipe out the leadership of tribes other than his own, resulting in thousands of deaths. Amin has ordered noncitizen Asians to leave the country and has expelled other foreigners he does not like. Kissinger explains that, while Europeans and Americans remain in Uganda, their numbers have declined, and the Soviet presence is expected to rise. The author expresses the opinion that US interests in Uganda are limited. Kissinger is a diplomat, author, political scientist, and Nobel Peace Prize recipient. He served as assistant to the president for National Security Affairs from 1969–1975 and as US secretary of state from 1973–1977.

The purpose of this memorandum is to bring you up to date on what is happening in Uganda and what actions we and others have taken. The nature of our future relations with Uganda is presently being reviewed. . . .

Henry A. Kissinger, "Memorandum for the President," *Foreign Relations of the United States, 1969–1976*, vol. E–5, part 1, Documents on Sub-Saharan Africa, 1969–1972, Document 261. Reproduced by permission.

Tribalism at Its Worst

Since his assumption of power in January, 1971, General Idi Amin has been destroying the elite of all tribes not allied or belonging to his own grouping. The judiciary, top civil servants, academics, the limited professional class and senior army and police officers have been Amin's targets. Amin has not had to eliminate whole tribes to insure his control; he has simply eliminated their leadership with little regard for the consequences of wiping out the economic and intellectual backbone of the country.

There are no reliable estimates of deaths. They most probably number several thousand but not above 10,000 in a population of 10 million. This compares with over 100,000 deaths in Burundi where the population was 3.5 million.

If Amin succeeds, his West Nile tribal kinsmen, who represent between 5 and 10% of the country's population, would rule the country. The ill-fated invasion of Uganda by Tanzanian-backed Ugandan dissidents has greatly strengthened Amin and accelerated the elimination of any opposition to him.

The Asian Expulsion

Amin's expulsion of Asians is moving apace. Most non-Ugandan Asians should be out of the country by the November 8 [1972] deadline. These appear to number 25,000 to 30,000, which is far less than earlier estimates of 55,000 expellees. Furthermore, Asians are not being brutalized as they were in the initial stages of the expulsion, probably because of the world's outcry, which included many African leaders.

Europeans and Americans in Uganda

As security deteriorated in Uganda, the number of Europeans and Americans resident there declined from an estimated 11,000 in September to 7,800. Our own presence went from 1,000 to about 700; all of our 114 Peace Corps volunteers were withdrawn. The British went from an estimated 7,000 to 5,000 citizens.

Ugandan president Idi Amin ruled during the 1970s and was responsible for the death and displacement of thousands of people. © Bettmann/Corbis.

The safety of Europeans and Americans does not appear to be a problem right now. Amin has resorted to expelling those foreigners he dislikes and otherwise, has told his troops to lay off whites, whose services the country still needs. In fact, Amin has gone out of his way lately to be friendly to the United States and West Germany, in the hope that we will respond with aid. (For all practical purposes, US aid to Uganda is presently suspended although we have not stopped on-going technical assistance. This subject is now under review.)

The Soviet and Arab Presence

Whereas most everyone else—excluding the French, whose presence has remained at about 200—has reduced its presence, our Embassy in [the capital of] Kampala expects the Soviet presence to rise above the present 125. This could result in Sino-Soviet competition between the Soviet-backed Amin versus the Chinese-supported [President Julius] Nyerere of Tanzania. It is too early to speculate on this subject.

A Case of Raw Tribalism: A 1972 Intelligence Information Cable to the US Government

[The Ugandan elite] are being eliminated because they, and the tribes of which they are the leaders and favorite sons, pose a threat to the continued control of Uganda by [Idi] Amin's own tribe, the Kakwa, and his West Nile allies. . . .

If [Amin] has not already done so, he may be able to consolidate his hold and keep it indefinitely. The Acholi, with originally the greatest strength in the army and police and, according to their claims, the greatest martial tradition of any tribe in Uganda, have let themselves be selectively slaughtered to the point that they will soon have no leadership left. The Lango never had a chance; they had made themselves so thoroughly hated during the [Milton] Obote period that the other tribes were quite happy to stand by and see them cut to ribbons by the West Nilers. The Itesot are somewhat of an enigma. There are still many of them in the army. They have apparently been so bemused by watching their ancient enemies the Lango and the Acholi get it in the neck, that it has not occurred to them that they might be next. Except for the Baganda, none of the other tribes appear to have enough strength to be a problem for Amin. . . .

What is happening now in Uganda has nothing to do with colonialism, nationalism, or east-west ideology. It is raw tribalism at work, with the chief of a minor tribe . . . on his way to subjugating and controlling the neighboring tribes.

National Archives, Nixon Presidential Materials, NSC Files, Box 746, Country Files, Africa, Uganda, vol. I.

In addition, a Libyan contingent (possibly 400 men) remains in Uganda. Both the Egyptians and Libyans have promised Amin assistance, which can only anger Nyerere, who, up to now, has blindly supported the Arab cause against Israel.

Future Actions by Amin and US Interests

Assuming Amin will remain in power, and both [the Department of] State and [the] CIA so believe, it seems likely that Amin will continue to purge Uganda's elite along tribal lines. He is also expected to pursue Africanization programs which will include the takeover of businesses vacated by Asians as well as probable future nationalizations affecting the British. Foreign missionaries will probably also come under increasing scrutiny by Amin.

Our own interests in Uganda are limited to protecting our remaining citizens and maintaining a presence in Uganda, rather than giving free rein to the Soviets, assuming they are responsive to Amin. However, if aid is a prerequisite for a presence, we may not be able to stay in Uganda.

The Government of Idi Amin Commits Gross Human Rights Violations

Whitney Ellsworth

The following viewpoint documents the testimony given in 1978 by Whitney Ellsworth before the Subcommittee on Foreign Economic Policy of the US Senate Committee on Foreign Relations. Ellsworth details Amnesty International's concerns about the human rights situation in Uganda. Idi Amin's military government put an end to the rule of law, government security officers routinely committed murder, and torture became the norm. The basic human rights guaranteed in the Universal Declaration of Human Rights were being denied, Ellsworth explains. The regime, however, chose to ignore international concern expressed about its elimination of almost all fundamental human rights. The Ugandan people were being terrorized, he asserts, causing many thousands to leave their homes and flee the country. At the time this testimony was given, Ellsworth was the publisher of The New York Review of Books *and the former chairman of the board of the US section of Amnesty International.*

Amnesty International is . . . extremely concerned about the human rights situation in Uganda. Since the military

Whitney Ellsworth, "Uganda: The Human Rights Situation," Hearings Before the Subcommittee on Foreign Economic Policy of the Committee on Foreign Relations, US Government Printing Office, 1978. Reproduced by permission.

government of President Idi Amin came to power by coup d'etat [sudden overthrow of the government] in 1971, a consistent pattern of gross human rights violations has developed and is still continuing.

Amnesty International's main concerns are as follows: (1) The overthrow of the rule of law; (2) the extensive practice of murder by government security officers, which often reaches proportions of massacre; (3) the institutionalized use of torture; (4) the denial of fundamental human rights guaranteed in the Universal Declaration of Human Rights; and (5) the regime's constant disregard for the extreme concern expressed by international opinion and international organizations such as the United Nations, which results in the impression that gross human rights violations may be committed with impunity. . . .

The focus is on events during 1977 and the first part of 1978. . . .

The aim of our report is not simply to deliver another condemnation of one man at the center of this terrible structure, who has been instrumental in creating and perpetuating it; what Amnesty International considers more important is to describe the whole structure, which involves many other individuals and which penetrates all areas of Ugandan society. The effect of this structure of repression can be said, without exaggeration, to have transformed the whole society in a short period of time into a ruthless military dictatorship marked by arbitrary arrest, torture, murder, the removal of virtually all fundamental human rights, the terrorization of the population, the turning of tens of thousands of Ugandans into refugees. . . .

The Overthrow of the Rule of Law

I will proceed briefly with our specific concerns. First is the overthrow of the rule of law.

After Uganda's military government came to power, Parliament was abolished, political parties were suspended, and Presidential rule by decree was enacted.

Constitutional safeguards against the misuse of power were reduced. A series of decrees signed by President Amin as chairman of the defense council directly conflict with the rule of law. First, the security forces have wide powers of arrest without warrant, and can detain indefinitely without charge any person suspected of subversion. Second, the security forces have immunity from prosecution, which was made retroactive to the beginning of military rule.

Third, any security official is empowered to "use any force he may deem necessary" to arrest or prevent the escape of anyone suspected of kondo-ism, which is armed robbery, which carries the death penalty. This supports a policy of shooting to kill on mere suspicion.

Fourth, military tribunals, originally confined to judging cases within the armed forces, are empowered to try civilians accused of capital offenses, such as sedition, subversion, or treason. This removes the possibility of obtaining a fair public hearing by an independent and impartial tribunal.

Under the Economic Crimes Tribunal Decree of March 25, 1975, economic crimes such as overcharging, hoarding, smuggling, corruption, fraud, embezzlement, illegal currency sales, et cetera, carry a maximum death penalty and are to be judged by a military tribunal.

The Security Forces: Disappearances and Killings

Next we turn to disappearances and killings by the security forces.

Since 1971, a very large number of persons in Uganda have disappeared following arrest by the security forces. A number have managed to flee the country when hearing of their imminent arrest, but the vast majority are never seen alive again. Only a very few survive the initial period of detention, and there is rarely any genuine judicial investigation of their cases leading to a court appearance.

Nearly all are tortured severely. Most torture victims either die under torture or are killed in other ways.

Ugandan president Idi Amin's army killed thousands of political prisoners during his brutal regime in the 1970s. © AP Images.

The arrests are carried out by different branches of the security forces, which normally take victims to their own headquarters. The various security agencies are as follows: The police; the army; the military police; the Public Safety Unit—this is a uniformed and plainclothes police unit, reportedly about 2,000 strong, set up in 1972 to deal with armed robbers: PSU night patrols regularly shoot on sight at suspected armed robbers and many persons have been killed by the PSU, allegedly "resisting arrest." Last is the Bureau of State Research. This is the much feared state intelligence agency, reportedly about 3,000 strong. Its headquarters are at Nakasero, Kampala, where many people have been tortured and killed since 1976, with very few survivors.

Persons arrested by officers of any of these security agencies are liable to summary executing by shooting or other methods, which have become common in Uganda. For example, a detainee may be ordered at gunpoint to murder other detainees by hitting them on the head with a hammer, axe, or car axle. In one version of this grotesque and common method of killing, detainees are lined up; the first man is given a hammer to kill the next man; he then in turn is killed by another man, until the whole line is killed, the last survivor being shot.

Bodies of those murdered are sometimes returned to relatives, usually in a mutilated condition, on payment of large bribes to security officers, of anywhere from $300 to $1,000. Many bodies are never recovered. Within the climate of fear inside Uganda, people do not readily divulge that relatives have disappeared or have found refuge in other countries. Even when refugees have reached other countries, they are usually afraid of contacting organizations, such as Amnesty International, for fears of reprisals against their relatives.

People Targeted for Arrest and Death

The cases known to Amnesty International are clearly a small fraction of the total number of people who have disappeared and been killed.

However, to present an overall view of the pattern of these killings, we detail in the written testimony the cases of people killed in the last 18 months for belonging to the various categories of the population which have become especially liable to arrest and death. I will mention here a few of those categories and cases.

First is politicians and civil servants. Large numbers of former parliamentarians and politicians have been killed, ranging from members of the former President [Milton] Obote's cabinet to several members serving as ministers under President Amin. All members of President Amin's original cabinet have been killed or have fled to exile.

Next are religious leaders and followers. The killing of the . . . Archbishop of the Church of Uganda, Rwanda, Burundi, and Boga-Zaire, is well known. But also there have been reports of ordinary church people being shot or arrested for contributing to the church celebrations or for wearing a badge commemorating the 1977 Church of Uganda centenary.

In October-November 1977, about 400 Christians in the Masaka region, mainly Catholics, were arbitrarily killed or arrested by soldiers.

Writers are another category. . . . [The] director of the Uganda National Theatre was arrested together with playwright John Male and John Sebuliba, Under Secretary of the Ministry of Culture, and they were sentenced to death by secret tribunal on July 23, 1977. They had been arrested at the opening night of John Male's play, "The Empty Room," which allegedly insulted President Amin.

Foreigners are another category particularly liable to execution and arrest. Citizens of several African countries have been arrested and many of them killed. . . . Citizens of other nations, including the United States, the United Kingdom, and the Federal Republic of Germany have also experienced arrest. . . .

Three Americans, named as Richard [Sanke], George Milton Smith, and Orson Brown were reported disappeared after arrests by state research officers on August 10, 1977, in a Kampala hotel. A Ugandan nurse, Monica Nansamba, later reported that she had been forced to behead their dead bodies in Mbuya Military Hospital.

Next is killings of members of particular ethnic groups. Members of former President Obote's ethnic group, the Lango, and the adjoining Acholi have been especially subject to killings since 1971. There were several massacres of Acholi and Langi soldiers in the army in 1971 to 1973 and again in 1977.

This last numbered 7,000 by some accounts.

Such incidents of large-scale attacks on members of one particular ethnic group might seem to suggest a case for examining whether this would not amount to genocide, which is an international crime.

Arbitrary Arrests, Killings, and Torture

Arbitrary and random arrests and killings also take place all over the country. Many persons have been arrested and killed simply because a security official or soldier decided to possess their wife, their house, their car, their property or shop, their cattle, their coffee crop, et cetera.

Because of this destruction of the rule of law, the most serious human rights problem in Uganda is that of killings committed by or acquiesced in by government or security officials. The estimates of the numbers of people killed since 1971 vary enormously. The lower limits do not go below 50,000 and the upper limits are anywhere around 300,000 or above.

Amnesty International is unable to verify these estimates.

Now let us consider the institutionalized use of torture. Following arrest, victims are usually taken to one of these detention centers where torture is almost routine, especially at three of them: Naguru, the public safety unit barracks; Nakasero, the headquarters of the bureau of state research; and Makindye, the military police barracks.

Many senior officers have been personally involved in torturing, according to several former victims and eyewitnesses. . . .

Geoffrey Mugabi, a Ugandan, described how he had been arrested on February 7, 1977, and taken to Makindye prison where he heard the noise of prisoners being strangled and their heads smashed. "The floors were littered with loose eyes and teeth," he said, and he had been forced to load the battered, bodies into trucks. On February 18 he had seen many trucks full of arrested soldiers who were then taken to the elimination cells, rooms C and D. He managed to escape. . . .

Violations of the Articles of the Universal Declaration of Human Rights

Let me turn briefly to other human rights issues in Uganda which are of concern to Amnesty International. Clearly these are minor in comparison to the massive violations already described. However, the full structure would be incomplete without a brief mention of the totality of violations of the Articles of the Universal Declaration of Human Rights.

I will summarize three of the many concerns.

The right to freedom of opinion and association have been completely removed in Uganda.

The right to freedom of religious belief is violated by the ban on certain religious sects.

There is no freedom of the press. The press in Uganda is totally government controlled or censored.

In conclusion, before President Amin came to power, the human rights situation in Uganda gave cause for concern. However, the scale of human rights violations changed dramatically after he came to power. Widespread arbitrary arrest, detention without trial, torture, and large-scale killing by the security forces were not isolated occurrences, but regular and systematic practices, condoned or encouraged by the Government. The rule of law was rapidly destroyed.

Reactions of the Amin Regime

One of the most disturbing aspects of the situation in Uganda is the fact that the Government has repeatedly ignored expressions of international concern and appeals on behalf of political prisoners. The Ugandan Government has taken no steps to improve the human rights situation. Internal investigations have been totally ineffective.

Uganda is a member of the United Nations Commission on Human Rights, but at the same time the Uganda Government consistently and with apparent impunity denies the most basic human rights guaranteed in the Universal Declaration.

In April 1978, President Amin announced a Uganda Human Rights Committee would be set up to "monitor all information in Uganda concerning human rights and coordinate with the U.N. Human Rights Commission. The committee would comprise officials of the Ministries of Justice, Defense, Internal Affairs, and Foreign Affairs, and of security organizations like police, special branch, and the state research bureau."

Since the security organizations are accused of responsibility for torture and killing, and since even judges can face reprisals if they conflict with the military regime, such a committee can have no independence or impartiality.

In January 1978, on the seventh anniversary of his regime, President Amin declared that 1978 would be a year of peace and reconciliation. He stated that there were no violations of human rights in Uganda and that such allegations were false propaganda by exiles.

Amnesty International is, however, convinced that this is not the case and that human rights violations continue. Though there have been periods in late 1977 and 1978 when political killing has diminished in intensity, the pattern of arbitrary arrests, disappearances, tortures, killings, and violations of fundamental human rights persist unaltered.

The Terror and Killings Inflicted by the Army

Patrick Moser

In the following viewpoint, journalist Patrick Moser reports in a 1984 military publication that under President Milton Obote, there was more terror, persecution, and death in Uganda than in the 1970s when the cruel dictator Idi Amin was in power. Human rights were grossly violated. Most of the blame fell on the army; it was almost totally undisciplined and out of control—killing, mutilating, and raping indiscriminately. Moser writes that army barracks and detention centers once again became houses of brutal torture and death. Those remaining in the transit camps set up by the army typically starved to death or were shot. Moser has served as a reporter, editor, and bureau chief for the news agency United Press International.

In Uganda the terror continues. Some people say it is worse now than during the murderous regime of dictator Idi Amin.

U.S. Assistant Secretary of State for Human Rights Elliot Abrams in August [1984] openly criticized President Milton Obote's human rights record in Uganda as "horrendous."

Patrick Moser, "Uganda: Still a 'Theater of Death,'" *Stars and Stripes* (European edition), September 20, 1984, p. 13. Copyright © 1984 by United Press International. All rights reserved. Reproduced by permission.

U.S. officials say up to 200,000 have died at the hands of the army in the past three years. Other sources put the toll of slaughter even higher.

AID [US Agency for International Development] workers in the troubled Luwero Triangle [area north of the capital city of Kampala] believe more people have lost their lives in the past two years than during the entire rule of Amin, once considered the worst butcher to ever rule an African country.

An Army Policy of "Premeditated Genocide"

Uganda has been a theater of death almost since independence from Britain in 1962. Much of the blame is laid at the door of the army, which has been unable to come to terms with increased guerrilla activity in the southern third of the country.

One AID worker charged that the army has engaged in "a policy of premeditated genocide by starvation." Other AID workers, residents and diplomats support this view.

They believe that the unstable situation following Amin's downfall severely worsened with the death in a fiery helicopter crash last December of Armed Forces Chief of Staff Gen. David Oyite Ojok. . . .

With Ojok's death . . . the 15,000-man army has been virtually leaderless. There has been an almost complete breakdown in discipline.

The army's victims are usually Bagandas, a southern Ugandan tribe of Bantu origin. Most soldiers are from the Nilotic tribes in the north of the country.

Evidence of Persecution and Murder

A doctor in Luwero said he recently saw some 1,000 troops drive to the villages of Kiwugo, Kimali, Sembwa and Unyangattan. . . .

"The first wounded arrived around noon—three children aged 11, 6 and 5, and a man, all with severe bayonet wounds," he said.

The following day a team of doctors went to the villages.

"We found the imprints of the soldiers' boots in the mud, two people wounded and at least 20 dead, including two women who were murdered together with their babies on their backs.

"One of the dead men was still holding an open Bible. Three houses had been burned, some of the bodies were partially calcinated," said the doctor.

Kampala residents cited the late May massacre of civilians and clerics at the Namugongo martyr's shrine 15 miles (20 km) east of the capital, which followed the sabotage of a nearby satellite communications station.

AID workers and residents said the 300 soldiers, unable to track down the saboteurs, turned on the local population, raping young girls and killing at least 90 people, including a number of seminarians.

Witnesses said the troops roasted a pig, forbidden and unclean meat to a Moslem, inside Namugongo mosque and wiped their hands on the Moslem holy book, the Koran. They also desecrated the nearby Catholic and Protestant shrines.

In a national radio broadcast, the government later apologized for the army excesses and arrested a soldier. It admitted to only 16 deaths.

"These killings at Namugongo fit into a pattern of persecution," said Paul Semogerere, leader of the official opposition democratic party.

"This persecution has grown over the years in harshness and brutality," he said.

A "Scorched Earth" Policy

In the *London Observer* newspaper in late August journalist William Pike said he spent 10 days in Uganda with the National Resistance Army [NRA], the main rebel group, and was shown numerous dumping grounds for bodies around Kampala.

He said residents told him army interrogations of suspected NRA supporters accounted for thousands of deaths.

"On some days 200 civilians were questioned and only 10 survived," he quoted army deserter Jackson Kekikomo as saying.

"We have been given orders to kill anything living: human beings, cows, dogs, hens," he quoted Pvt. Fastine Itadal, captured by guerrillas in February, as saying. "This is called scorched earth."

Places of Torture, Starvation, and Death

Army barracks and detention centers have regained the notoriety they had under Amin's regime.

"One should not forget that the infamous torture chambers used by Amin had been built by Obote before he was overthrown as president by Amin in 1971. So when Obote came back to power in 1980, he found them in good working order," an expatriate doctor said.

"Only a few prisoners managed to get any food," said a former detainee at Makindye barracks near Kampala who is now in exile. "Every morning at about 7 the officer in charge would ask the same question: 'How many have died?'"

Sometimes up to 30 a day died in that cell, the detainee said. Their bodies, especially those with signs of torture, were loaded onto trucks and dumped in the bush.

Until three months ago, AID workers said, there were 165,000 people in transit camps, set up by the army in a bid to cut local support for the NRA.

The government earlier this year said as many as 750,000 people had been displaced by army sweeps. Recently a number of these camps were closed and the villagers sent back to their homes.

"When they got there they found nothing," said one AID worker. "The army had stolen their cattle and burned their fields and houses. Even the Red Cross convoys taking food and blankets for these people were looted by the army."

(In January guerillas kidnapped 11 Red Cross workers near Luwero but released them unharmed 18 days later.)

"Those who still remain in the camps—which are nothing else than extermination camps—are either shot or left to starve," the AID worker said. "It is a policy of premeditated genocide by starvation. The idea of this genocide is the extermination of the Baganda tribe."

Resettlement in the Luwero Triangle After Years of Terror

Blaine Harden

In the following viewpoint, US journalist Blaine Harden reports on the violence and fear that caused residents to flee Uganda's Luwero Triangle during the 1980–1985 conflict. The Triangle was a prosperous and fertile farming region until conflict between government and rebel armies ravaged the land and its residents. After five years of conflict characterized by killings and unmitigated brutality targeting the Baganda people especially, Harden writes, a new government came to power, and people began to return to what was left of their old homes. United Nations programs and aid from other countries helped the returnees make a new start. Harden was Washington Post *bureau chief in sub-Saharan Africa from 1985 to 1989. He is the author of the 1990 publication* Africa: Dispatches from a Fragile Continent.

Livingston Sendindikawa is back in town. But, as the burly farmer readily admits, he does not cut the prosperous figure that he once did in this coffee-trading village [Kapeka, Uganda]. All that he has left after two years of running and hiding from government soldiers is a shredded pair of trousers, a shirt, a machete and a farm overgrown with elephant grass.

Gone are his six acres of coffee and banana trees—chopped down by soldiers. Gone are his furniture, his beds, his linen, his radio, his dishes, his bicycle, his kettle, the iron roof over his house, his front door—stolen by soldiers. Gone are his 40 cattle, 20 chickens and four goats—shot, butchered and eaten by soldiers. Gone are his wife and one of his six children—killed by soldiers, Sendindikawa says, while his family was on the run.

The rampaging soldiers have since fled. They were chased away last year by the rebel National Resistance Army (NRA), a fighting force that does not kill civilians, shoot their chickens or steal their cooking pots.

The government of Yoweri Museveni, the former NRA leader and now Uganda's president, has appealed to the U.S. government and other foreign donors to help farmers such as Livingston Sendindikawa. He is one of tens of thousands—a precise number is not known—of Ugandans who have walked back home in recent months and begun to put their farms and their lives back together.

The Luwero Triangle: Once the Center of Horrific Fear and Violence

Kapeka is in the heart of Uganda's Luwero Triangle, an extraordinarily fertile farming region north of the country's capital of Kampala. Before the violence began here, about 1.5 million people lived in this 10,000-square-mile area that once had one of the highest standards of living in East Africa. There were coffee farms and automobiles, houses with electricity and schools with glass windows.

But during the 1980–85 rebel war against the regime of former President Milton Obote, a guerrilla conflict that started here in these lush farmlands, the Luwero Triangle became the center of government retribution.

"The violence was horrifying," said Gary Mansavage, an official for the U.S. Agency for International Development, which

A man kneels in a Luwero farm before the skeletal remains of genocide victims in 1986. © Time & Life Pictures/Getty Images.

has taken the lead among foreign donors in financing reconstruction here. Mansavage said that the outside world has been slow to grasp the scale of the killing that took place here.

"In South Africa in the past two years, about 1,900 people have been killed. In Luwero in four years, about 200,000 were killed," Mansavage said.

Reports of mass killings in the area were made public in mid-1984 by the U.S. State Department. They were denied, however, by the Obote government and subsequently discounted by the British government.

As proof of what the Luwero Triangle endured, returning farmers in the past six months have collected the unburied skeletons of thousands of their murdered relatives and neighbors and stacked them on roadsides across the region.

"We have decided not to bury these people, they have been put on display as witness to the death," said the Rev. Grace Kalyowa, an Anglican priest in the town of Nakaseke.

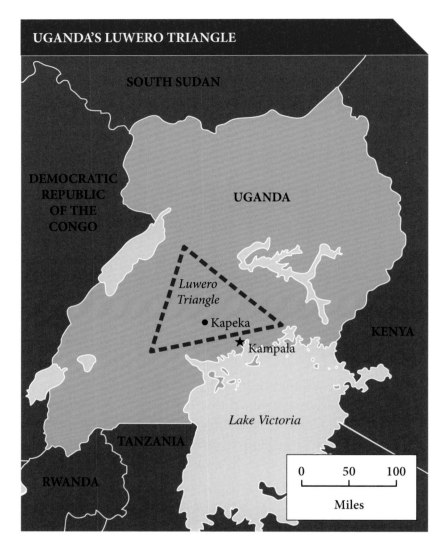

UGANDA'S LUWERO TRIANGLE

SOUTH SUDAN

DEMOCRATIC
REPUBLIC
OF THE
CONGO

UGANDA

*Luwero
Triangle*

● Kapeka

KENYA

★ Kampala

Lake Victoria

TANZANIA

RWANDA

| 0 | 50 | 100 |

Miles

The priest conducts guided tours of an abandoned four-story hotel in Nakaseke that until last summer was a center for torture and murder. Soldiers in Obote's government, most of them members of the northern Acholi tribal group, rounded up members of the local Baganda tribe for interrogation in the hotel.

The walls of the hotel are covered with graffiti, scrawled by government soldiers before they fled, that denounce Museveni and threaten the Baganda people. An example: "A good Muganda is a dead one shot to kill."

"Baganda people were thrown off the roof of this hotel. If you refused to say 'yes,' you were involved with the rebels, you were thrown down," said Kalyowa, who said he saw several people thrown from the hotel's roof. "Inside, they used to drip melted plastic [from plastic bottles] onto people's skin. They also used to cut off flesh of people to the bone to make them talk."

Aid for Returnees

The level of brutality and fear was such, according to international aid officials, that it was several months after Museveni's January takeover of the government before former residents of the Luwero Triangle began to filter home. Many families sent "scouts" to see if the region was indeed rid of the Acholi soldiers.

The initial trickle of returnees has turned into a flood, according to the Kampala office of the U.N. Children's Fund, which is spending $1.8 million to drill wells for drinking water for returnees. UNICEF said there were about 2,800 people living in the Nakaseke district in March, but that by the end of May there were 45,000 people.

"If people are initially set up with good water, they can very quickly prosper. This is a very fertile area," said Eamonn Marrett, an engineer supervising the drilling of the UNICEF wells.

AID, whose past involvement in Uganda has been limited, has begun a five-year $18.2 million loan program to help revive agrobusinesses, such as coffee processing plants and tanneries, in the Luwero Triangle. It also is seeking approval for a $6 to $7 million loan program for small farmers. The program would loan returning peasant farmers between $68 and $1,000 to buy the hoes, machetes, seeds and chickens that could get them started again.

"People are coming back and taking charge of their lives. Many of them will harvest a crop in four months or so," said Emily McPhie, an AID official with responsibility for the Luwero

Triangle. "It is very reasonable that with a little capital they can become productive farmers in a short time."

However, the flow of U.S. and Western European foreign aid to the Luwero Triangle in recent months has not kept up with returnee demand, according to local government officials in the subcounty of Kepeka.

Joseph N. Kazinna, a member of the local NRA governing committee, said the area is in urgent need of medicines, gasoline cans and cooking pots.

The Renewal of Human Rights Abuse in Uganda

Colin Nickerson

In the following viewpoint, journalist Colin Nickerson reports on events that made people fear Uganda was reverting to its old policies of brutality and abuse of human rights. He explains that when Yoweri Museveni took power in 1986, he promised, among other things, peace and respect for human rights. A little more than a year later, Nickerson details, incidents of killing, cruelty, torture, and looting rose, especially in the northern area of the country. There, in the name of revenge, youthful soldiers of the National Resistance Army perpetrated the same kind of horrors the new government promised to end. Nickerson is a foreign correspondent for the Boston Globe.

North of [the capital city of] Kampala lies a lush region known as the Luwero Triangle. So fecund is the soil of Luwero, a local saying goes, that a man who plants a mango seed in the morning will feast on fruit from a full-grown tree that afternoon.

But the earth yields more than sweet mango.

Salim Mukumbe, 22, who says he fled the region in terror after government troops murdered most of his family in 1984, returned this past spring to reclaim his family's small farm.

As he plowed his field one day recently, every new furrow revealed a terrible bounty of human bones—brittle sections of spine, yellowed femurs, broken ribs protruding from the loam. And skull after hollow-socketed skull, each horribly grinning, each punctured by bullets or crushed by blows.

Mukumbe simply plowed under the femurs, the vertebrae, the rib bones. But the skulls he added to a large pile by the edge of his land. And each time he would cover his face with his hands and murmur a short prayer.

"I have seven relatives in that bone heap," he said. "I have a father, two brothers, a sister and three uncles in that bone heap."

The Luwero Triangle was the scene of almost unimaginable butchery during the first half of the decade as the soldiers of former President Milton Obote slaughtered tens of thousands of peasants suspected of sympathizing with the National Resistance Army, or NRA, the main rebel faction seeking to depose him.

When the NRA—headed by an idealistic guerrilla chief named Yoweri Museveni—seized power in January 1986, it seemed that Uganda's long nightmare might be over.

Dashed Hopes for Change

But today there are signs that Uganda is reverting to its bloody old ways.

"Again we are seeing the killings, the brutality against civilians, the torture," said John Owina of the Uganda Human Rights Activists, a monitoring group. "The abuses are not yet widespread. There is still hope. But the worm is in the fruit."

Upon claiming victory, Museveni vowed that Uganda would make a break from its gruesome past. Corruption would be rooted out, human rights respected, and the ragtag remnants of Obote's army—still fighting in the northern provinces—crushed once and for all. Peace would descend upon the long-suffering nation like a blessing.

For awhile, at least, it seemed Museveni might be able to keep that promise. His disciplined young troops, many not even in their teens, quickly restored order to the capital, Kampala, and surrounding areas. For the first time in years, peasants who had fled to neighboring countries started returning to Uganda's fertile fields.

"Uganda seemed to be coming back to life. There was a tremendous sense of hope, of possibilities," said a Kampala-based official of a Western relief agency, an individual who has worked in Uganda on and off for nine years.

But now, the relief official said, "The country is teetering on the edge, and the tilt seems to be back toward chaos."

A Return to Violence

Come evening, the gunfire begins in Kampala. Usually just isolated shots fired by nervous soldiers. But sometimes rocket-propelled grenades streak down dark streets with a terrifying whoosh. One exploded recently next to the compound of the French volunteer medical group, Médecins Sans Frontières.

"Who knows who is firing, or why?" said one of the French doctors. "It might be soldiers, it might be insurgents. Or it might be some foolish lorry driver with a grievance. This poor country has more weapons than people."

One night recently there was a brief but intense firefight in a residential section just a few blocks from downtown Kampala. Muzzles sparked and red tracer rounds arched in seeming slow-motion through the hot, humid air. There came an explosion. Then screams. Then silence.

Asked the following day about the battle, an army officer said, "Perhaps it was bandits."

Almost from the day it gained independence in 1962, this former British colony—which [British prime minister] Winston Churchill once described as "the pearl of Africa"—has suffered under brutal tyrants, most notably Obote and Idi Amin, and faced civil wars spawned by deep-rooted tribal rivalries. There has long been animosity between the Acholi and Langi tribes of the north and the Baganda and other Bantu-speaking people of the south.

It is believed that more than 500,000 Ugandans were killed under the regimes of Obote and Amin, mostly by undisciplined soldiers and by the secret police of the dreaded State Research Bureau.

The Deteriorating Discipline of the NRA's Boy Soldiers

Museveni, a former schoolteacher, took to the bush in 1981 to form the National Resistance Army. He started out with 27 followers who shared 23 Kalashnikov rifles. Five years later, the NRA—by then thousands strong—captured Kampala, although it still has not gained full control of the countryside.

Many of Museveni's soldiers were children. A common sight during the fierce battle for Kampala was that of an 8- or 9-year-old NRA fighter struggling with a rocket launcher or other weapon larger than himself. Many of these boy soldiers—as they came to be called—were orphans whose parents had been killed by Obote's troops. Their cause was vengeance.

Today the once-vaunted discipline of Museveni's youthful soldiers appears to be deteriorating. "The army of liberation has become an army of occupation," said a Western diplomat. "Museveni is basically a naive militarist. His intentions are good. He is honest. But those years in the bush taught him only how to topple a government, not how to run one."

On a steamy morning recently, the roadblock on the road from Entebbe to Kampala was manned by 13-year-old soldiers with 100-year-old eyes. They carried AK-47 assault rifles and were teetering drunk—eyes red with alcohol, breath stinking of same. While one rummaged through the bag of a reporter, two others methodically kicked a prisoner who lay on the ground, wrists manacled behind his back.

"The man is a thief," said the first soldier with a shrug.

Blood was streaming from the prisoner's ears and nostrils, but he made no sound. The boy soldier demanded a cigarette, then waved the reporter on; a boot heel smashed the prisoner's jaw.

A Return to the Brutality of the Past

Such shakedowns and public brutality were common during the Amin and Obote eras but almost unheard of until recently under NRA rule.

But even more troubling are reports of torture, looting and even murder by government forces.

"The NRA is now committing the very atrocities it came to power to prevent," said Owina, the human rights activist.

Most of the reported instances of brutality have occurred in northern areas where the government faces a widening insurgency by Acholi tribespeople still loyal to Obote.

"Obote's Acholi army killed so many Ugandans," said Owina. "The NRA soldiers want revenge. They think it is their turn to kill and torture and imprison. But if Uganda is to survive, we must find a common ground that is not a killing ground."

In Kampala, the army barracks atop Kololo Hill, used during the Obote government for the torture of political prisoners, is now serving the same purpose, according to human rights activists. Dozens of prominent political figures have been jailed on charges of subversion. . . .

Western diplomats, meanwhile, are worried by Uganda's growing links with Libya's Moammar Khadafy. It was Khadafy who supplied the bulk of the weaponry with which the NRA shot its way to power. According to diplomatic sources, Soviet-built Antonov cargo planes bearing Libyan markings make regular night landings at Entebbe Airport, disgorging loads of war materials.

Kibali—A Town of Ghosts

The fighting between NRA forces, most of whom belong to the Baganda tribe (Museveni is from the small western Ankole tribe), and the Nilotic tribes of the north has been concentrated in the Gulu and Kitgum districts on the border with Sudan. But there have been small clashes within 20 miles of Kampala.

In Kibali, a village located within the Luwero Triangle, brilliantly flowered creeper vines curl through the bullet-pocked ruins of the schoolhouse. Every store is roofless, every wall bears shrapnel scars, every church is defiled by explosives.

"This town is no longer a town—it is a place of ghosts," said Fred Ddlumulia, a 30-year-old schoolteacher who returned here recently. He holds classes near one of the ubiquitous skull piles beside a dirt track. "That is what Uganda has become, a land of ghosts."

"No one wants war. We Ugandans are sick and tired of war," he said. "We pray to God for peace. But sometimes I think God does not love Uganda."

The National Resistance Movement Government's Failure to Safeguard Human Rights

Amnesty International

In the following viewpoint, a 1992 Amnesty International report examines the human rights record of Yoweri Museveni's National Resistance Movement (NRM) government. The report states that the NRM made some improvements in regard to human rights after it came to power in 1986. But uprisings by rebels in north and east Uganda led to a new pattern of major human rights violations, including massacres by the army of unarmed civilians and prisoners, unlawful detention in army barracks without charge, and torture. The report explains that the government used such charges as treason to hold suspected critics or opponents; often such charges were false—with no evidence to support them. More often than not soldiers involved in human rights violations while on active duty were not brought to trial. Amnesty International is an independent international organization that works to protect human rights around the world.

Uganda was a devastated country when the National Resistance Army took power in January 1986. It had been torn apart by civil war and 20 years of political violence. Human rights had been persistently and grossly violated. The economy had been ruined.

The National Resistance Movement (NRM) government, led by Yoweri Museveni, took charge of this devastation, promising to build a new Uganda with respect for human rights central to its program. Since then, breaking with the past has been a dominant slogan in Ugandan politics.

Several early government actions indicated that the NRM intended to translate its stated commitment to human rights into practice. In areas firmly under NRA control, jails were opened and the arbitrary harassment, killing and torture of civilians largely stopped. The government set up new institutions and posts: a Human Rights Commission to investigate the past and an Inspector General of Government (IGG) to investigate corruption and human rights violations in the present. It ensured that Uganda was among the first states to accede to the United Nations (UN) Convention against Torture and Other Cruel, Inhuman or Degrading Treatment or Punishment (3 November 1986) and moved quickly to ratify the African Charter on Human and Peoples' Rights (10 May 1986).

The New Pattern of Human Rights Violations

Almost immediately after taking power, the NRM government faced armed opposition in the north and east, and since the second half of 1986, a new pattern of serious human rights violations has emerged in Uganda. Massacres of unarmed civilians and prisoners by soldiers of the government's National Resistance Army (NRA) have taken place every year. The victims have included children and whole families. Some have been burned to death in their homes; others have suffocated to death after being crammed into pits or other confined places of detention. Yet others have been beaten or shot to death by soldiers who apparently believe they are above the law. Thousands of people have been unlawfully detained without charge in military barracks where many have been tortured or ill-treated. The authorities have also misused serious charges such as treason to hold suspected opponents or critics of the government.

Government officials frequently blame these violations on the legacy of the past or invoke Uganda's history to suggest that, relatively speaking, the human rights situation is better than before. From these and other similar responses, it appears that the government is prepared to use the past as a smokescreen to hide both its own complacency and, in some instances, the deliberate and cynical violation of human rights by high-ranking military and government officials. However, neither the past nor comparisons with the past can ever excuse or justify the continuation of gross human rights violations in the present.

Many of the most serious violations of human rights have taken place in the north and east of the country in the context of counter-insurgency operations and appear to be connected to the government's counter-insurgency strategy. But violations, particularly detention without charge or trial and torture, have also taken place in Kampala and other areas of Uganda less affected by conflict.

The Need for a New Approach to Punish Human Rights Violations

The government has been under pressure to mount prompt, independent and impartial investigations into the many extrajudicial executions committed by soldiers since 1986. Where particularly blatant incidents have taken place or publicity has been brought to bear, the government has claimed, often long after the incident, that investigations would be set up or were already under way. However, in the vast majority of cases, investigations have been neither independent nor impartial, their progress has been unacceptably slow, and none has issued a report that has been made public.

The government frequently points to its willingness to execute soldiers as an indication of its commitment to human rights: over 40 soldiers have been executed since 1987. The death

Yoweri Museveni (center) assumed the presidency of Uganda in 1986 under the National Resistance Movement party. © AP Images/Ronald Kabuubi.

penalty is mandatory in Uganda for serious crimes against the person such as murder or rape under both the Penal Code, which governs all citizens, and the Military Code, which regulates the behaviour of soldiers. Trials under the Military Code are unfair as they do not allow a right of appeal.

The government claims that the death penalty is an effective deterrent against human rights crimes despite the fact that Uganda's entire history suggests that it is not. Moreover, its belief that the death penalty is a deterrent and that soldiers must be ruled by violence appears to be a barrier to political decision-making about fundamental and effective reforms to protect human rights. Its stated belief in the most serious of punishments must also be thrown into question by its inconsistent use of punishment in general, particularly in relation to human rights crimes. While soldiers found guilty of committing abuses off-duty have frequently been summarily tried and executed, few soldiers implicated in human rights violations during military operations have been brought before the courts. Action has also been public and prompt when soldiers, even senior officers, are suspected of corruption or theft. The failure to act in a similar way in relation to human rights crimes suggests that the use of terror is a deliberate counter-insurgency tactic and that in these situations such violations may be condoned by the government at a high level.

In addition, false or draconian charges have been laid against real and suspected critics and opponents of the government, including prisoners of conscience. There has been widespread use of the charge of treason to justify remanding prisoners in custody, in effect using it as a holding charge in the absence of substantial incriminating evidence. In many cases political prisoners have been detained without charge for months, sometimes years, and have then been charged with treason, preventing their release on bail for a further 16 months. Charges of sedition or defamation have been used against journalists who criticize the government or army and, in a case in April 1992, against a defence lawyer in a high-profile treason trial.

Insurgents fighting the NRA in both northern and eastern Uganda, some of whom were members of pre-1986 government armies responsible for gross human rights violations, have also committed serious human rights abuses. Civilians, including villagers who refuse to supply rebels with food, suspected government informers and members of locally recruited militia and their relatives have been abducted, raped, murdered or mutilated by insurgents in the northern districts of Kitgum and Gulu. In eastern Uganda, in the districts of Kumi, Soroti and Pallisa, civilians, particularly elected councillors, have been victims of deliberate and arbitrary killings by armed opposition groups. These abuses deserve and receive widespread condemnation both in Uganda and outside. They do not, however, justify human rights violations by the NRM government and the army.

Positive Steps Taken by the Government

Some government action in relation to human rights issues has brought results. In 1987, for example, a cruel form of tying, known as three-piece or kandooya [tying victims' arms behind their backs and gradually tightening], was banned throughout the NRA, and the ban appears to have been widely respected. This demonstrates that when the political will is there, the authorities can take effective action. Nevertheless, other forms of torture and, occasionally, kandooya are still reported to be taking place.

Other positive steps have included the release in 1989 and 1990 of over 4,800 uncharged detainees arrested in rural areas in the north and east. Many had been held without trial for up to three years. In 1992 there are significantly fewer people in uncharged detention but, again, many arrests since 1990 demonstrate that the army is quick to resort to unlawful detention if soldiers think there is a need to put people in custody, and detainees still have access to no better safeguards against arbitrary detention than in the past.

In the early years of the NRM government, the legacy of past eras meant that violent incidents were almost inevitable. Individuals had many scores to settle and it would have been unrealistic to expect the government to break immediately the cycle of violence entrenched in Ugandan society. But after six years of rule by the NRM it is, at the very least, questionable whether human rights violations are the result of a legacy of disorder. The tragedy of Uganda's past would only be compounded if it has become a convenient excuse for human rights violations perpetrated in the present.

Terror in the Name of the Lord

Bob Drogin

In the following viewpoint, journalist Bob Drogin reports on the atrocities committed in northern Uganda in the mid-1990s by the Lord's Resistance Army (LRA) and provides insight into the actions of its leader, Joseph Kony. He explains that the LRA's goal was to overthrow the government of Ugandan President Yoweri Museveni and replace it with one that would enforce the Ten Commandments. Much of the cruelty and brutality inflicted on villagers by the LRA was based on Kony's superstitions and whims, Drogin writes. To help ensure a future generation of followers, Kony abducted young women and married them off to LRA soldiers. Although the government sent out army troops to stop the LRA, they were not successful in their efforts. Drogin is a Pulitzer Prize winner, a former foreign correspondent for the Los Angeles Times, *and an author.*

Brig. Gen. Chefe Ali, army commander of the north, held his gleaming cavalry sword high as he mounted his steed—in this case, the back of a bicycle pedaled by an aide—and charged off into the bush here [Amuru, Uganda] last week to inspect the depredations of Africa's latest nightmare.

For two hours, terrified villagers told Ali of atrocities and attacks by the Lord's Resistance Army, a fanatic Christian fundamentalist cult led by a self-proclaimed prophet with a murderous manner.

Okeya Santo recounted how the rebels shouted, "Teachers come out!" when they came to his hamlet late last year [1995].

When the 32-year-old schoolteacher emerged from his hut, they shot him in the chest and both arms. "I said, 'You are killing me for no reason,'" Santo recalled, his right arm now amputated at the elbow. "They said: 'You are a teacher. We don't want teachers.'"

On March 22, the guerrillas returned. This time they burned 17 thatch-roofed huts and the local school. Four villagers stepped on land mines left by the retreating rebels: One was killed, and three lost limbs.

Lord's Resistance Army (LRA) leader Joseph Kony (left), pictured with his deputy Vincent Otti, carried out a reign of terror in northern Uganda that garnered worldwide attention in 2012. © AP Images.

In Topiny Marinus' charred hut, someone left a message scratched on the mud bricks: "This war will not end."

That much is clear. Since stepping up their attacks in early February [1996], members of the Lord's Resistance Army have killed at least 250 people, mostly civilians, and abducted hundreds more in this Central African nation. They say their goal is to topple the government of President Yoweri Museveni and to install a regime dedicated to enforcing the Bible's Ten Commandments.

The State of Affairs in Some African Countries

Brutal and bizarre insurgencies are hardly new in Africa, where rebels without a coherent ideology have laid waste to Sierra Leone, Liberia, Somalia and other nations in recent years. Civil wars and military demobilizations have left others flush with guns and unemployment, while soldiers have turned to banditry from Zaire to Nigeria.

Some governments, of course, have been even worse. Here in Uganda, hundreds of thousands of people were tortured, imprisoned and killed during nearly two decades of rule by dictators Idi Amin and Milton Obote.

Museveni has led his long-suffering country into the modern world since he seized power in 1986. The economy is now the fastest-growing in Africa, the press is free and presidential elections are scheduled for May. Foreign donors and investors have poured in more than $1 billion in hopes that Uganda's long years of tyranny and terror are finally over.

Joseph Kony and His Lord's Resistance Army

But Uganda's progress, at least in the north, is now held hostage by a former Roman Catholic altar boy named Joseph Kony and his Lord's Resistance Army.

"They kidnap, they kill, they rape and they maim," said a senior Western diplomat in Kampala, the capital. "They're like the Four Horsemen of the Apocalypse when they come in." . . .

Kony's LRA is an outgrowth of the Holy Spirit Movement, a Christian cult that ravaged northern Uganda in the late 1980s. It was led by Alice Lakwena—a nom de guerre [assumed name] that means "messiah"—who claimed she was possessed by the angry spirit of a long-dead 95-year-old Italian soldier.

Kony, reportedly Lakwena's cousin, emerged as her successor after she went into exile in 1988. He too claimed he was controlled by spirits. But backed by officers once loyal to Obote, Kony soon eclipsed his mentor, at least in terms of cruelty and sheer bizarreness.

At first, his troops routinely sliced the lips, ears or arms off their victims. Later, anyone seen riding a bicycle or owning white chickens was slain. These days, the owners of white pigs are killed.

Kony said he cut off lips to stop people from reporting his whereabouts. Similarly, in an area without phones or cars, he targeted bicycles to stop riders from warning authorities. And chickens?

"White chickens are allegations," scoffed Walter Lutkang, a former LRA guerrilla captured by the military. "What he doesn't like is pigs. Pigs are ghosts."

Kony's Tactics and Power

In a world where superstition is a large part of reality, such tactics barely raise an eyebrow. But others do.

The army says, for example, that Kony's men cut up a teacher in Kococh village in 1991 and cooked his remains in a saucepan. "They said the children should eat him," Ali said. "But [the children] said, 'No, kill us first.'"

A grainy video shot in January 1994, when Kony met a Ugandan official for unsuccessful peace talks, shows a tall, thin man in his early 30s with huge aviator sunglasses and gaily beaded braids that dangle to his shoulders. His voice, bellowing through a bullhorn held by armed bodyguards, is mesmerizing.

Betty Bigombe, a state minister who met Kony six times in those talks, says he can barely write his name. But she doesn't

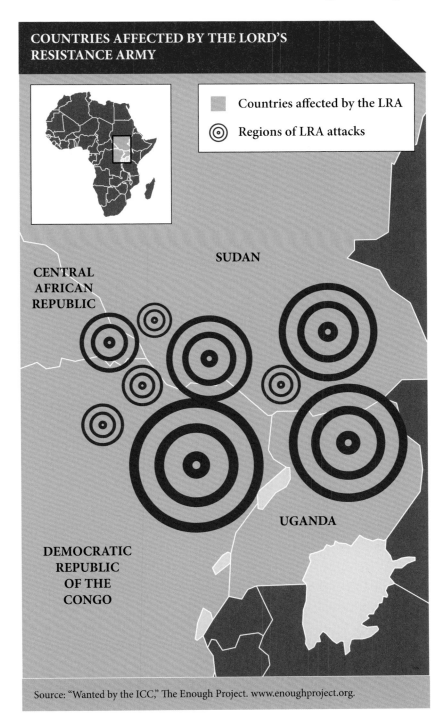

COUNTRIES AFFECTED BY THE LORD'S RESISTANCE ARMY

Countries affected by the LRA

Regions of LRA attacks

SUDAN

CENTRAL AFRICAN REPUBLIC

UGANDA

DEMOCRATIC REPUBLIC OF THE CONGO

Source: "Wanted by the ICC," The Enough Project. www.enoughproject.org.

underestimate his power. "He controls the minds of his followers," she said.

From Altar Boy to Bigamist and Abductor of Young Women

By all accounts, Kony was an altar boy and catechist as a youth. Later, he became a traditional healer. It's a potent mix: Today he claims he talks to God and has his troops smear a local nut oil on their chests in the shape of a cross to protect them from bullets.

Kony delivers bitter prophecies in daylong sermons, sometimes shaking and speaking in tongues. His chief lieutenant is called Hitler. And Kony sometimes wears women's dresses, perhaps as a disguise. He has 32 wives.

Deserters and escapees from Kony's press-ganged army say Kony abducts young women and forces them to marry LRA soldiers. "He wants a new generation of his followers," said one. "That's why he marries [off] all the girls."

An Abductee's Story

Agnes Oroma, 20 and shy, said she was ordered to marry an LRA captain after she was kidnapped from Pabo village in June [1995]. With 450 other captives, she was forced to march for days across the desolate wilderness to an LRA base camp in Sudan— whose Islamic fundamentalist regime reportedly provides arms and support to Kony and his troops.

"They said I was to be trained as a soldier," she said softly. "They said we should fight to spread the word of God."

Anyone who tried to escape was killed, Oroma said. Religion pervaded military life. "To salute, we say, 'Praise the Lord,'" she said.

Oroma hiked back to Uganda on Feb. 28 [1996] as part of the LRA's new offensive. She decided to run away when her husband beat her for refusing to carry his assault rifle as well as her own.

"Men don't carry anything," she complained. As for Kony, she said, "he doesn't fight himself."

Oroma and about 85 other former abductees are now interned at a Ugandan army base in Gulu, the provincial capital. Also at the base are hundreds of sets of Sudanese fatigues, assault rifles, machine guns, grenades, bazookas, land mines and other ordnance that the army says it captured from the LRA.

The Battle Between the LRA and the Ugandan Army

For now, the estimated 400 to 800 guerrillas in the LRA are unlikely to rout the government in Kampala. About 20,000 soldiers, or half the army, have been sent to stop them. New helicopters and night-vision equipment are expected and should aid their task.

But the battle is not going well. On March 8, the LRA machine-gunned and burned a 17-vehicle convoy of civilian cars and buses. The military says 22 people were killed; survivors insist that more than 100 died.

"The soldiers escorting us in front, they just ran off on foot without firing," bus driver Yaya Bilali, 58, said bitterly from his hospital bed. He was shot in the buttocks and leg as he tried to follow, and then was relieved of his watch by an LRA guerrilla who found him bleeding in the bush.

In a similar attack last week, the LRA ambushed a truck in northern Uganda, killing all 15 people inside, newspapers reported Sunday.

On March 13, the rebels fired a mortar at St. Mary's hospital, the nation's second largest, outside Gulu, and set land mines by the entrance that killed one woman and wounded two others.

"This is basically a child army that is terrorizing the people," said Dr. Matthew Lukwiya, deputy medical superintendent. He complains that the army has "no sense of urgency" because only civilians are attacked.

That might change. Tuesday night [March 26, 1996], a large LRA force attacked an army outpost for the first time, wounding three soldiers. In an apparent escalation Friday, the rebels attacked a key northern military barracks and destroyed at least

90 civilian homes, the army said. No military or civilian casualties were reported.

Ali, the bicycle-riding army commander, insists he is making progress. But he is frustrated. The rebels run rather than fight, he complains. They attack at night, when helicopters are useless. And they strike where least expected.

"We have been working a long time without achieving very much," he added sadly.

An Attack on Homosexuality

Saeed Ahmed

In the following viewpoint, journalist Saeed Ahmed discusses Uganda's Anti-Homosexuality Bill proposed in 2009. Homosexuality was already against the law, and 95 percent of the people wanted it to remain so. If the proposed bill passed, anyone convicted of having gay sex would go to prison for life, while anyone testing positive for HIV or taking part in homosexual sex more than once would face a death sentence. The "promotion of homosexuality" would be forbidden as well. Many Ugandan Muslim and Christian religious leaders favored passage of the bill; human rights groups wanted Western countries to cut off aid to Uganda if the bill passed. Saeed Ahmed is the supervising news editor at CNN Wire.

As a gay man in Uganda, Frank Mugisha is used to the taunts, the slurs and the daily harassment of neighbors and friends.

But if a new bill proposed in the east African country becomes law, Mugisha could be put away for life, or worse, put to death for having sex with another man.

"Right now, you can't go to places that are crowded, because the mob can attack us or even burn us. We can't walk alone. We

Saeed Ahmed, "Why Is Uganda Attacking Homosexuality?," CNN, December 8, 2009.

The Background of the Anti-Homosexuality Bill of 2009

On September 25, 2009, MP [member of Parliament David] Bahati introduced the Anti-Homosexuality Bill, his first-ever piece of legislation. News reports have suggested that the legislation was not homegrown but the result of a conference held in Kampala, Uganda in March 2009 with U.S. evangelicals. The conference, which drew thousands of Ugandans, focused on how to convert homosexuals into heterosexuals. . . .

Under the Ugandan Penal Code, any person who has "carnal knowledge of any person against the order of nature" commits an offense that is punishable by life in prison. . . . Despite the fact that it is rarely enforced, the law serves as a justification for discrimination, harassment, and the denial of government services. Homosexuals face harassment in public spaces, expulsion from schools, and discrimination in employment. There have also been high-profile asylum cases of homosexual Ugandans fleeing persecution.

are ostracized by relatives. But if this bill passes, it will become impossible for me to live here at all. And that part hurts the most," Mugisha said.

Five Provisions of the Anti-Homosexuality Bill

The Anti-Homosexuality Bill features several provisions that human rights groups say would spur a witch hunt of homosexuals in the country:

- Gays and lesbians convicted of having gay sex would be sentenced, at minimum, to life in prison
- People who test positive for HIV may be executed
- Homosexuals who have sex with a minor, or engage in

Furthermore, a misconception exists that homosexuality itself is illegal. As one scholar writes:

[I]t is not illegal to be a homosexual nor is it illegal for men to kiss, live together, or take any other action short of intercourse. . . . however, people throughout the country seem to have taken this to mean that it is illegal merely to be homosexual. . . .

MP Bahati's legislation, however, proposes to take the existing laws and policies a step further. According to its preamble, the purpose of the bill is to "protect the cherished culture of the people of Uganda, legal, religious, and traditional family values of the people of Uganda against the attempts of sexual rights activists seeking to impose their values of sexual promiscuity on the people of Uganda."

Lucy Heenan Ewins, "The Criminalization of Sexual Orientation: Why Uganda's Anti-Homosexuality Act Threatens Its Trade Benefits with the United States," Boston College International and Comparative Law Review, *vol. 14, 2011, pp. 149–151. http://lawdigitalcommons.bc.ede.*

homosexual sex more than once, may also receive the death penalty
- The bill forbids the "promotion of homosexuality," which in effect bans organizations working in HIV and AIDS prevention
- Anyone who knows of homosexual activity taking place but does not report it would risk up to three years in prison

"Who will go to HIV testing if he knows that he will suffer the death sentence?" Elizabeth Mataka, the U.N. Special Envoy on AIDS in Africa, told reporters last week [December 2009]. "The law will drive them away from seeking counseling and testing services."

Ugandan Reactions to the Bill

Homosexuality is already illegal in Uganda under colonial-era laws. But the bill, introduced in October, is intended to put more teeth into prosecuting violators.

It applies even to Ugandans participating in same-sex acts in countries where such behavior is legal.

"They are supposed to be brought back to Uganda and convicted here. The government is putting homosexuality on the level of treason," Mugisha said.

Lawmakers have indicated that they will pass the bill before year's end.

It has the blessing of many religious leaders—Muslim and Christian—in a country where a July poll found 95 percent opposed to legalizing homosexuality.

The Rev. Esau Omara, a senior church leader, said over the weekend that any lawmaker opposing the bill will pay for it during the next election, according to local newspaper reports.

And a leading Muslim cleric, Sheikh Ramathan Shaban Mubajje, has called for gays to be rounded up and banished to an island until they die.

Several media outlets also have inflamed sentiments in recent months by publicly pointing out gays and lesbians.

In April, the *Observer* newspaper published tips to help readers spot homosexuals. And over the summer, the *Red Pepper* tabloid outed 45 gays and lesbians.

Uganda's President Yoweri Museveni has not publicly stated his position on the bill, but last month blamed foreign influence in promoting and funding homosexuality.

"It is true that, if the president has said that, he must have information that European nations are promoting (homosexuality) and recruiting homosexuals," government spokesman Fred Opolot said. "You must note that the president or the legislators are responding to the concern of the citizenry of the country."

Ugandan gay rights activist Frank Mugisha stands in front of a portrait of US politician Robert F. Kennedy. Mugisha was awarded the Robert F. Kennedy Human Rights Award in 2011 for his work in gay rights in Uganda. © AP Images/Haraz N. Ghanbari.

Western Reactions to the Bill

At the Commonwealth summit in Trinidad and Tobago late last month, Canadian Prime Minister Stephen Harper said he pulled aside Museveni to deplore the bill.

"We find them inconsistent with, frankly, I think any reasonable understanding of human rights, and I was very clear on that with the president of Uganda," Harper told reporters.

In the United States, a coalition of Christian leaders released a statement Monday denouncing the bill.

"Regardless of the diverse theological views of our religious traditions regarding the morality of homosexuality, in our churches, communities and families, we seek to embrace our gay and lesbian brothers and sisters as God's children, worthy of respect and love," the statement read.

Human rights groups have called on Western nations to withhold aid from Uganda if the measure passes. About 40 percent of the country's budget comes from international aid.

"This draft bill is clearly an attempt to divide and weaken civil society by striking at one of its most marginalized groups," said Scott Long, director of the Lesbian, Gay, Bisexual and Transgender Rights Program at the New York-based Human Rights Watch. "The government may be starting here, but who will be next?"

Opolot, the government spokesman, said consideration of the bill in parliament is merely "democracy at work."

"We as a country are engaging and debating a pertinent issue," he said. "So if a foreign country chooses to cut aid simply because Uganda is debating its destiny, then it is quite outrageous and quite wrong."

Mugisha, who now heads the group Sexual Minority of Uganda, said he is working with lawyers and other activists to change minds and defeat the measure.

"I have put a lot of effort in this struggle. I just want to live freely every day," he said. "I want to be happy knowing that if I'm going to meet someone, I'm not going to be taken to jail forever."

Editor's Note: As of early 2012, Uganda's Anti-Homosexuality Bill had not become law.

CHAPTER 2

Controversies Surrounding Uganda

Chapter Exercises

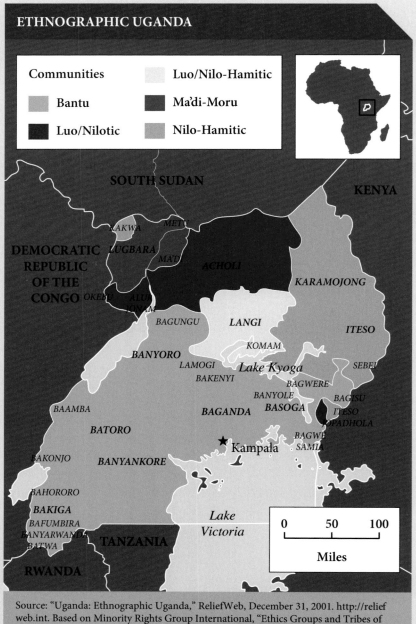

ETHNOGRAPHIC UGANDA

Communities

Bantu

Luo/Nilotic

Luo/Nilo-Hamitic

Ma'di-Moru

Nilo-Hamitic

SOUTH SUDAN

KENYA

DEMOCRATIC
REPUBLIC
OF THE
CONGO

KAKWA   METU

LUGBARA

MA'DI   ACHOLI

KARAMOJONG

OKEBU   ALU
JONAM

BAGUNGU   LANGI

ITESO

BANYORO   KOMAM

LAMOGI   Lake Kyoga   SEBEI

BAKENYI   BAGWERE

BANYOLE   BAGISU

BAAMBA   BAGANDA   BASOGA   ITESO
OPADHOLA

BATORO   BAGWE
SAMIA

BAKONJO   BANYANKORE   Kampala

BAHORORO

BAKIGA   Lake
Victoria

BAFUMBIRA

BANYARWANDA   TANZANIA

BATWA

RWANDA

0   50   100

Miles

Source: "Uganda: Ethnographic Uganda," ReliefWeb, December 31, 2001. http://relief
web.int. Based on Minority Rights Group International, "Ethics Groups and Tribes of
Uganda," *Uganda: The Marginalization of Minorities*, 2011.

1. Analyze the Map

Question 1: Which community occupies the greatest amount of territory in Uganda?

Question 2: To which community do the Langi belong? The Iteso?

Question 3: Which part of the country—north or south—is home to the Acholi?

2. Writing Prompt

Assume you are a Ugandan citizen during a time period of your choosing and write an editorial expressing your views about whether or not the West should use its economic power to influence the way the Ugandan government treats its people.

3. Group Activity

Form groups and debate the following statement: The Ugandan government has invited the International Criminal Court to investigate wrongdoing, so the court has already lost its impartiality.

Multiple Factors Were at the Root of the Expulsion of Uganda's Asians

Meir Amor

Some historians have explained the 1972 expulsion of Asians from Uganda as an inevitable part of that nation's transition to political independence. Sociologist Meir Amor maintains in the following viewpoint that the inevitability argument is too simplistic. He argues in favor of a broader approach to the issue, one that integrates such socio-historical factors as ethnicity and class animosity between Africans and Asians. He also takes into account how independence and modern citizenship affected groups' identity, and he focuses on contemporary political circumstances of independent Uganda. Ugandan Asians, he points out, were the second, not the first victims of large-scale violent ethnocentrism in independent, postcolonial Uganda. He views the expulsion of the Asians by Idi Amin as "an act of legalized, public robbery by a state of its defenseless subjects." Amor is an associate professor of sociology at Concordia University in Montreal, Canada.

When Ugandan Africans acquired political independence in 1962, so the argument goes, Ugandans of African origins lumped the British and the Asians in the same package as

Meir Amor, "Oppression, Mass Violence and State Persecutions: Some Neglected Considerations," *Journal of Genocide*, vol. 4, no. 3, September 2003, pp. 370–376. Copyright © 2003 by Taylor and Francis Group. All rights reserved. Reproduced by permission.

economic and cultural colonial exploiters. Therefore, the expulsion of the Asians from Uganda was an inevitable part of the African anti-colonial movement and an assertion of political independence of a self-reliant, post-colonial African state. Being few, vulnerable, and unable to retaliate and constituting "nobody's problem," the Asians were a much easier target than the British colonial masters.

I take an issue with such an historical portrayal of inevitability and with this "natural-rational" theoretical explanation. As [African specialist] Michael Twaddle avers, the inevitability claim rests on an ". . . economically unjust, sociologically illiterate, and historically unsound" analysis. In addition, I would argue that the inevitability argument is [an] affirmation that focuses on Asians' economic exploitation and social exclusiveness as if these factors were the only social causes at the root of [Ugandan president Idi] Amin's expulsion of the Uganda Asians. Not only does it indirectly condone Amin's action and victimize the victims again, but it also suggests a sterile economic interpretation. . . .

What is needed, therefore, is an approach that integrates socio-historical factors such as ethnicity and class antagonism between Africans and Asians and among Africans. Secondly, such an approach should consider the effect independence and modern citizenship had on groups' identity. Thirdly, it should focus on contemporary political circumstances of independent Uganda. Against such a background, the idiosyncrasies of [Ugandan president] Milton Obote's unitary state revolution and, especially, Idi Amin's brutal regimes of terror can be contextualized and the expulsion of the Asians might be comprehended. Furthermore, I would argue that the economically oriented focus on the Asians' Ugandan history . . . has a major historical flaw: it ignores the crucial fact that the Ugandan Asians were the second victims of violent ethnocentrism in Uganda. The first victimized group in post-colonial and independent Uganda was Ugandan Africans: the Bagandas. That is, the people of the province and kingdom of Buganda.

Bagandas: The First Victims

Bagandas were victimized in 1966. They were politically sub-jugated by their own state's army. Their king, who was also the president of Uganda according to the independence agreement signed under British auspices, was expelled from Uganda. The 1962 agreement constituted a constitutionally federated Uganda. The 1966 violent actions were carried out by the Ugandan army ordered by Milton Obote, the first Ugandan Prime Minister. The army's assault on Buganda was led by one of the army leading Generals: Idi Amin. Therefore, an attempt to explain the ethnic violence that erupted in Uganda against the Asian minority necessitates weighting the possible political effects independence and citizenship might have had on ethnic and class antagonism within the independent Ugandan state and society.

In 1967, Milton Obote, by now the only ruler of Uganda, promulgated a new constitution in which the federal structure of post-colonial Uganda was completely eradicated. Milton Obote established a unitary state. It was a state in which no autonomous provinces were recognized. All the previous ethnic and sub-national identities of the peoples comprising Uganda were formally and officially obliterated. Uganda became a centralized state. . . . The new centralized state presumably recognized as its citizens Ugandans, regardless of their previous, continental, local, and tribal or kingdom cultural heritage. . . . Obote demolished the very distinct nature and cultural legacies which were the center and the backbone of Africans' identities within the imposed British political structure of the Protectorate. Obote's centralized state implemented to the fullest extent the British colonial project of the Protectorate of Uganda—the very "Uganda" which was nothing but a colonial artificial designation imposed on the various peoples living in that part of East Africa.

However, in January 1971 the Ugandan army ousted Obote by a military coup. And in August 1972, 20 months later, the Ugandan Asians were ordered to leave the Second republic of

Uganda, now ruled by President Idi Amin. Hence, Ugandan Asians were the second, not the first, victims of large scale violent ethnocentrism in independent, post-colonial Uganda. . . .

Ugandan Asians: The Second Victims

Between 1894 and 1972 the Asians' ethnic minority in Uganda became economically successful, socially segregated and politically isolated. This state of affairs positioned Uganda Asians in a constant vulnerable position. Their economic achievements were based on a shaky political ground. During the Protectorate years it was completely dependent on the political (good) will and economic interests of the ruling British bureaucracy, and, since independence, on the protection of the Ugandan state. With Uganda's independence and the transfer of power to the hands of Ugandans of African origins, the conflict between Asians and Africans became open, exposed and declared. Moreover, state institutions unequivocally favored the African citizens' economic and social interests. Citizens of Asian origins were treated as second class citizens by their state. . . .

The anomalous situation of Asian Ugandans after independence was represented by two central issues that were on the daily agenda in Uganda. The first was the issue of *Ugandan citizenship*. The second was concerned with the economic and political policies of *"Ugandization versus Africanization."*

Ugandan Citizenship: Ugandization vs. Africanization

The issue of Ugandan citizenship brought to the fore not only the ambivalent stand of Uganda Asians concerning their civil status in Uganda, but also the different notion of citizenship prevalent among Uganda's Africans. With independence Asian Ugandans had three choices with which to resolve their ambiguous citizenship status. Formally they could become British or embrace Ugandan citizenship or return to India. Most Asian Ugandans wished and opted for British citizenship. This was the case despite

Ugandan Asians gather outside the offices of the British High Commission in Kampala in 1972, hoping to get travel documents for political asylum in Britain after being expelled from Uganda by Idi Amin. © AP Images.

the fact that during the late 1960s and early 1970s, England made many efforts to restrict their immigration to Britain. India did not welcome them and was considered to be a last resort after Ugandan citizenship. Those Asians who were born in Uganda were Ugandan citizens by birth. They had no options; Uganda was their state and home.

For those Ugandan Asians who accepted Ugandan citizenship *de facto* [in fact] or *de jura* [or, *de jure*, meaning legally] it meant tying up their fate permanently with the new Ugandan state. . . . Whatever decision Ugandan Asians had taken, it had a profound economic and political significance upon the relationships with the African Ugandan majority. . . . Questions of Asians' citizenship and loyalty were problematized with Uganda's independence. It acquired acute dimensions with Milton Obote's 1967 dictatorial constitution and with Amin's ascendance to state power in January 1971. . . .

To African Ugandans . . . the concept of citizenship was inseparable from the concept of kinship. The state rested on a principle of political consanguinity, a presumed descent from a shared forefather. This pristine conception shaped their modern history. . . . Biological intermingling and cultural assimilation were the only effective ways of entering such African citizenship. Ugandan Asians did neither. Not only did Asian Ugandans keep strict social, familial and sexual exclusiveness, they also fulfilled a conspicuous and exploitative economic niche. Amin's response to the Asians was rooted in his resentment toward the Asians' mode of social (cultural and economic) behavior. In addition, one should consider Amin's pressing political and economic needs. [According to author Dent Ocaya-Lakidi] Asians' attitudes and behaviors ". . . created the impression that the Asians are 'get-rich-immigrants-in-transit', without the interests of East Africa at heart." Amin, it seems, fully subscribed to these ideas. . . .

African kinship represented to Africans a cluster of mutual obligations such as responsibilities toward the old and the weak, fellowships, hospitality and solidarities on which African societies were founded. These characteristics were reflected in the Swahili notion of *Ujamaa*. . . .

The perception of Asian Ugandans' segregationist attitudes coupled with this kind of African perceptions of citizenship could not have found a more extreme manifestation than the one espoused by General Idi Amin Dada. Amin's charges against the Asian Ugandans were premised on their flagrant economic exploitative position and on their tendency for social exclusiveness. However, Amin could not see himself the "Dada" of "brown" Ugandans. Not only did Asians explicitly reject contacts with Africans, it was also African cultural perception that deepened the gulf between these communities. Class disparities, social suspicions and economic competition augmented and fed cultural hostilities. "The fact of the matter is," says Ocaya-Lakidi "that most black Africans have such a low opinion of Asians that they would not have wanted to associate too closely with them."

The Rise and Fall of Idi Amin

During the 1970s, the notorious Idi Amin blazed onto the scene and quickly developed a reputation for living large and conducting a loathsome campaign inside Uganda to purge it of his perceived enemies. . . .

Amin belonged to the Kakwa, a diverse group living in Uganda's northwestern region of West Nile. . . . Although ethnically from the north, Amin grew up in the south. Because of his size and strength, he shunned an education in favor of the British regiment known as the King's African Rifles. He was a vicious boxer and bullying leader, and quickly rose through the ranks to become a general. When [Milton] Obote took power, Amin was a logical candidate for military commander.

Amin . . . used his position to amass wealth and power and . . . replaced much of the army's command structure with his own and other ethnic groups from northwestern Uganda. . . . [In 1971] Amin staged a military coup. So began his brutal regime in which an estimated three hundred thousand Ugandans were killed in obscenely violent ways, their bodies tortured and mutilated. He methodically purged the professional classes, intimidated the intelligentsia, and

With the August 1972 expulsion decree, Asian Ugandans were radically excluded from Uganda's modern identity. . . .

Idi Amin Dada's interpretation of the African *Ujamaa* could not include Ugandan Asians. Asian Ugandans were expelled by the Ugandan state from the newly created Ugandan universe of obligation. Usurping state power, Amin, the President of the Second Republic of Uganda, "legalistically" terminated these relations with state-sanctioned ethnocentric violence.

Contributing Factors

With the 1962 Ugandan constitution, a federated, territorial citizenship was instituted. However, the various economic and po-then banished the Asian commercial community, seizing their properties and businesses and giving them ninety days to leave the country. Amin and his cronies took all they could steal. The economy eventually collapsed, schools and hospitals closed, roads deteriorated, and soldiers, loyal to Amin, roamed the countryside, slaughtering humans and wildlife with abandon.

In the process, Amin established himself as one of the world's most demented dictators by launching an outlandish lifestyle that included driving a bright red Italian sports car at breakneck speeds through the dirt-poor backcountry, hosting lavish feasts, and bragging that he and his men ate human flesh. . . . With his country in shambles, Amin did what bad leaders do to divert attention from their failures: he went to war. In late 1978, he invaded neighboring Tanzania over a minor border disagreement.

Any sense of victory was short-lived, however. In 1979, Amin's army crumbled in the face of a counter-invasion by the Tanzanian army and the Uganda National Liberation Army. . . . Amin fled to Libya, eventually settling in Saudi Arabia, where he died in 2003.

Peter Eichstaedt, First Kill Your Family: Child Soldiers *of Uganda and the Lord's Resistance Army.*
Chicago: Lawrence Hill Books, 2009, pp. 10–13.

litical policies enacted by Obote's regime to Africanize Uganda's economic and political structure brought to a head the complex colonial layers of ethnic conflicts within the Ugandan. . . . Africanization of the economy and politics of Uganda meant a deliberate policy of discrimination between Africans and non-Africans on the basis [of] nativity to the African continent and skin color. In short, Africanization meant racialization of the complex ethnic relations prevalent among the various cultural groups inhabiting the new nation-state of Uganda.

With Amin's seizure of power and after he reverted to kinship and ultimately to a racist definition of citizenship, institutional discrimination was legalized. . . . Asian Ugandans had no place in Amin's "citizenship." They had to go. . . . [In addition] not being able to deliver the economic goods he promised all Ugandans, Amin needed a readily available source of capital. The Asians were an easy target. . . .

Expelling the Asians was the beginning of an "economic war" during which Amin took possession of the British concerns in Uganda. The expulsion of the Asian was a symptomatic incident of Amin's lawless rule, but it was also a continuation of the ethnic and political hostilities among Ugandans of African descent.

The Ugandan Asians' social fate exemplified clearly the anomalous location of ethnic minorities in the middle. Their internal structure, in combination with the problematic relationships with their social environment, positioned them in a constant vulnerable stand. Despite their economic success their political weakness created a situation in which a policy of a "comprehensive solution" could be implemented against them. . . . Their side, weak and isolated politically, had no power to respond, let alone retaliate.

The expulsion of the Asians was an act of legalized, public robbery by a state of its defenseless subjects. The perpetration and full responsibility of the dictatorial regime, the speed and the comprehensiveness in which the anti-Asian policies developed to a general expulsion, not only highlighted the social and cultural acceptability of these measures, but also the unresolved conflicts presented to Ugandans by the notion of citizenship.

The Asians were chosen as a result of their vulnerability and the political needs of a tyrant with an army at his disposal. The fact that neither India nor England were ready to defend their former citizens deepened their vulnerability and augmented their helplessness. In other words, their vulnerability stemmed from the lack of protection and their victimization had only an indirect connection to their middleman status.

From Amin's point of view, the expulsion of the Asians served several political functions, including the will to "punish" Britain. The immediate booty was enormous, though the economic damage to Uganda's economy could not be even estimated. However, after October 1972 Uganda was practically empty or "free" of Asians. The crime Amin committed against the Asians was only part of his unrestrained crimes and destructive policies against Ugandan Asians and Africans alike. These policies got even bloodier until he was ousted from power in 1978.

The British Government Supported Idi Amin's Brutal Rule

Mark Curtis

In the following viewpoint, author Mark Curtis contends that Britain was well aware of Idi Amin's corruption, ruthlessness, and unsavory reputation and yet welcomed him and supported his regime to further its own interests. Britain was pleased about Amin's military coup because it improved British prospects in Uganda. British planners even went so far as to hope that pro-British forces elsewhere might initiate such coups in their own countries. Reports of killings and human rights abuses in Uganda notwithstanding, the British supplied Amin's regime with military and economic aid and continued to do so despite some officials' qualms. Almost to the end, they chose to conduct business as usual and rationalize what was happening in Uganda. Curtis is an author and journalist, a former research fellow at the Royal Institute of International Affairs, and director of the World Development Movement.

The coup by then Army Chief of Staff [Idi] Amin took place while [President Milton] Obote was attending a Commonwealth conference in Singapore and involved the arrest or shooting of officers loyal to Obote, resulting in the deaths of hundreds of people. The coup was immediately greatly welcomed by British officials. Britain was one of the first countries to formally recognise the new regime, along with the US and Israel, in contrast to some African states, such as Tanzania and Zambia, which refused to recognise the legitimacy of the new military regime. 'Our interest in Uganda in terms of citizens, investment, trade and aid programme . . . are best served in these circumstances by early recognition', the Foreign Office noted. . . .

The British welcome . . . came with no illusions about Amin's bloody past and character. Amin was 'corrupt and unintelligent', [assistant under secretary of state] Harold Smedley wrote two days after the coup. There was 'something of the villain about him and he may well be quite unscrupulous and indeed ruthless', a Foreign Office official wrote six days after the coup. . . .

There was a further hope expressed by British planners—that Amin's military coup might be replicated by other pro-British forces. Eric le Tocq of the Foreign Office's South East Asian Department wrote that: 'General Amin has certainly removed from the African scene one of our most implacable enemies in matters affecting Southern Africa. . . . Our prospects in Uganda have no doubt been considerably enhanced'. . . .

When this period is discussed at all in the media or elsewhere (which is rare), the standard line is that given how Amin soon expelled the Ugandan Asians, British planners must have made a 'mistake' in acquiescing in Amin's rise. This is not the case; British policy was far from being a 'mistake'. The fact is that Britain consciously supported and connived in the rise of Idi Amin precisely because of long-standing British interests to get rid of governments like that of Obote who were challenging 'elites' and promoting 'popular measures'. . . .

British Reaction to Terror in Uganda

The subsequent story of Amin's rule is one of repression and terror, a second phase that was in effect also supported by Britain as a brief chronology can show.

Ugandan president Idi Amin is carried by four British men into an official reception in 1975. The gesture was symbolic of Amin's ties with Britain. © AP Images.

By February 1971 Amin had 'concentrated all the powers of parliament and of the former President in his hands', the British High Commission in Kampala noted. He announced that elections would only take place in five years. One Foreign Official wrote that 'it is now beginning to look as if Uganda may merely have exchanged one form of authoritarian government for another'. In early March a decree banned all political activity for two years and people 'continue to be detained without trial'—the High Commission officials estimated that the number was around 1,000.

The British reaction was instructive. One Foreign Office official wrote that 'I can appreciate that a period of rule free from all politics, if that is in fact a genuine possibility, could be desirable'. The official went on to say, however, that a 'complete cessation' of politics for two years was 'unnecessary', before adding: 'I readily recognise that too much democracy in a country like Uganda at the present stage can be as fatal as too great a degree of authoritarianism. What would seem to be required for the foreseeable future is a realistic balance between firm and, indeed, authoritarian, government and some degree of democratic expression. I believe Uganda needs no necessarily democratic government, but it is important that government should be representative and fair as well as firm.'

With power being concentrated into Amin's hands and officials recommending 'authoritarian' government, the Ugandan regime approached Britain for arms. 'Armoured cars can go ahead. Strikemaster aircraft OK. Perhaps Harriers [a type of military jet],' wrote the Foreign Office's Eric Le Tocq. British policy, he said, should be to show a willingness to supply arms to prevent the Ugandans going elsewhere but discourage them from purchases which are 'overambitious, militarily, technically or financially'.

On 21 April a British 'Defence adviser' in Kampala met the Ugandan Defence Minister and subsequently reported that 'the prospects for defence sales to Uganda are both clearer and brighter'. . . . A Foreign Office official wrote that: 'We consider it important . . . both in order to keep his [Amin's] goodwill and also to assist in maintaining the stability of his regime that we should facilitate as far as we can the meeting of requests for equipment from this country'. Another official wrote of the 'political desirability of supporting General Amin'.

By mid-May, the High Commission was noting continued arrests with up to 1,000 inmates in one prison in Kampala. A further decree issued that month ordered that people could be detained with no time limit if ministers believed that they were engaged in subversive activities. The High Commission was also getting 'several reports' of incidents in which British subjects 'have fallen foul of the army'. In one, a senior expatriate civil servant was severely beaten and his Ugandan deputy beaten to death 'because it was thought that men working under him had been recruited for Obote'.

Military and Economic Matters

In early July Amin announced he wanted to visit Britain in the middle of the month to discuss British training of the Ugandan army and joint military exercises. The British government quickly arranged what was in effect a state visit. . . . It was understood that 'the primary purpose of General Amin's visit is to discuss military matters' as Amin met the Queen [Elizabeth II], the Prime Minister [Edward Heath] and the Defence Secretary [Lord Peter Carrington], among others.

The brief from the Foreign Office read: 'General Amin has abandoned Obote's radical pan-African policies for a more moderate and pro-Western policy'. The new government, a High Commission official wrote, was 'not ideal, but by African standards as good as could be hoped for'.

At these meetings Foreign Secretary [Alexander] Douglas-Home told Amin that 'we would help as best we could' on military and economic aid and with the training of troops, although supplying Harrier jets would be too costly for Uganda. A £2 million contract to supply 26 Saladin and 6 Saracens armoured personnel carriers was signed. The *Daily Telegraph* wrote in an editorial that General Amin was: 'a staunch friend of Britain. . . . His request now for the purchase of equipment for the rebuilding of Uganda's defences deserves the most sympathetic consideration from every point of view'.

These July agreements with the Ugandan military were being signed while hundreds of soldiers were being massacred by Amin's forces in Uganda. 'The killings took place at a large number of army camps across Uganda', a Foreign Office official wrote the following month. 'A large number of officers and men, in particular from the Acholi and Langi tribes (those associated with Dr Obote) were killed'.

Three days after this note, on 16 August, another Foreign Office official wrote that: 'From the point of view of British interests, General Amin's regime has so far served us well. He is extremely well-disposed to Britain . . . and his coup removed one of our more bitter African critics. We have already done much to assist in the establishment and recognition of his regime and we are doing what we can to help him overcome his present difficulties'.

By August Amin had announced the establishment of a military junta. In the same month, Britain offered a £10 million loan for three years. High Commissioner [Richard] Slater was saying that 'despite some obvious deficiencies, he remains a net asset from Britain's point of view'. Slater recognised that the Acholi and the Langi 'have fled or been killed or imprisoned', saying that 'this is the rather sombre background to a bright chapter in Anglo-Ugandan relations'. 'I am sure that he [Amin] is sincerely grateful for what we have done and offered to do', such as early recognition, military and police training and the financial loan. Slater added that: 'So long as he stays in power, Ugandan reactions to controversial British policies in Africa will be containable and the influence of the moderates in the OAU [Organisation of African Unity] will be strengthened. It remains therefore a British interest to see his regime consolidated'.

A Continued Willingness to Help

This basic support was being offered despite officials' 'misgivings . . . about the course Uganda is taking'. This included 'the continuing financial mess, with talk of expensive military equipment', the 'dangerous lack of civil law and order' and 'the internecine strife in the army that threatens the whole basis of his rule'. These were the beginnings of the eventual recognition that the Amin regime was so incompetent and corrupt that it was a liability. But this point had not yet been reached.

In November, the Foreign Office noted that 'power remains firmly in Amin's hands' and that 'he is probably ruthless enough to brook no opposition'. It envisaged further 'repressive measures' to 'add to the unspecified numbers of those who have disappeared or are held in prison without trial'. It also stated that 'the prospect is of a continuing slow drift towards bankruptcy and the gradual emergence of the less savoury aspects of a military dictatorship'.

Officials were also becoming increasingly wary of Britain being publicly identified with Amin. Britain's 'public and visible involvement with the regime' such as the military and police training teams and the visiting aid mission, meant that 'we might well be saddled with some of the criticism belonging to the Amin regime'.

One year into the regime's grip on power, in January 1972, Ugandan Defence Minister [Charles] Oboth-Ofumbi visited Britain to buy arms and was shown 'a wide range of military equipment' and given reassurances of 'our willingness to help'. 'The main obstacle as far as we could see concerned the provision of funds', British officials told him; any lingering human rights problems never appear to have been raised. . . .

By February 1972, High Commissioner Slater could amazingly say to the Foreign Office that he 'had no immediate bilateral problems to discuss' with Amin—a few hundred murders, the banning of all political activity and beatings of expat civil servants apparently not worthy of discussion with the despot now in control in Kampala. . . .

[Lord] Aldington [an emissary] met Amin on 24 March. Four days before, the Foreign Office noted that [High Commissioner] Richard Slater: 'confirms that during January anything up to 400 detainees at Mutukula were put to death in cold blood after appearing before some sort of kangaroo court. Mr Slater thinks that Amin must have known what was going on but acquiesced. . . . An unknown number of people appear to have been killed on 27 February at Soroti as a result . . . of army and police brutality'. The same note said that Britain should continue to help the country 'get out of the mess it is in' by economic aid and training missions.

Killings, Disappearances, and Business as Usual

Referring to the 400 deaths, another Foreign Office official noted that Amin may 'have to resort to more unpleasant manifestations of his power in order to retain authority, ie, more disappearances and deaths'. 'He may increasingly become an unsavoury friend to have'. This official also wrote: 'It is a nasty business and seems bound to excite international attention. We may well get some awkward parliamentary questions. . . . We are close to Amin and are known to be close to Amin and some of the odium may well rub off on us. If there are any more reports and if we get a spate of awkward questions, particularly if they refer to the help we are giving Amin, we may find it necessary to ask the High Commissioner to seek from Amin some explanation'.

Thus after mass killings and clearly announced decrees of repression, Whitehall [the British government] might simply seek 'some explanation' from Amin, which might only be necessary due to 'awkward parliamentary questions'.

The files show that by the early months of 1972 there were constant stories of killings by the army. . . .

[In] May an ex-MP [member of Parliament] and prominent lawyer, Anil Clerk was taken from his home by the police and was not heard of for weeks. The Clerk case received some press coverage in Britain, by which time the brutality of the Amin regime was public knowledge. At this point, Foreign Secretary Douglas-Home recommended sending 'a strong message' to the Ugandan government saying that the Clerk case could lead to a deterioration in relations.

But Clerk's disappearance promoted a rather extraordinary despatch by High Commissioner Slater. He wrote that: 'So now we know who we are dealing with. On the one hand, a man [i.e., Amin] of considerable charm, endowed with tremendous energy, concerned for the welfare of his people, well-disposed towards Britain. On the other hand, a tyrant, vindictive, ruthless, moody and stubborn as a child, often quite unamenable [sic] to reason, pathologically suspicious, a liar and hypocrite. On balance more Hyde than Jekyll, and not the man one would choose to do business with'.

But then, Slater argued, 'we do not have a choice'. 'We cannot tell him to stop murdering people' and 'my plea is for business as usual'. Slater argued that Britain could not conceivably influence Amin by withdrawing some measures of support and any move against him 'would be fraught with consequences for our community [i.e., the thousands of British passport holders in Uganda] for which we are at present ill-prepared'.

Foreign Office official Simon Dawbarn noted later that there were reports that 'Amin was personally responsible' for Clerk's death but that 'we must go on doing business with Amin' since 'we have too many hostages in Uganda', referring again to the British passport holders.

The Break

It was not until June 1972 that, according to the files, British officials began to consider cutting off support to the Amin regime. . . . His hold on the country seemed 'increasingly insecure' and the discipline of the army had deteriorated with killings continuing. 'The army is now feared by the civilian population', the Foreign Office noted. The military training team should be delayed since 'there would be a risk of criticism in the press and parliament which would not be easy to refute'. . . .

On 5 August Amin told the British High Commissioner of his intention to expel 80,000 Asian British passport holders from Uganda, giving them three months to leave, and accusing them of excluding Africans from business and being responsible for illegally exporting capital. [Prime Minister Edward] Heath wrote to Amin urging him to reverse this announcement saying that: 'The British government have gone out of their way to try to be friendly and cooperate with Uganda ever since your administration took over. We were and are very anxious to help you in all the economic and security problems which face your country. I have hoped that our personal relations could be close'.

Right up until the last, therefore, British ministers were obsequiously trying to deal with this dictator. Even then, the files show that officials wanted to retain the British army training team in Uganda—'we thought that it was doing useful work and we did not want the current differences between our two governments to broaden', the Foreign Office noted. It was Amin who expelled the team in September as British officials then spoke of a break in diplomatic relations.

The West Has the Power to Affect Events in Uganda

Richard H. Ullman

In the following viewpoint, written in 1978, professor Richard H. Ullman argues that events in Uganda should have been condemned. The West should have taken the lead, he writes, as very few African leaders were willing to speak or act publicly against Idi Amin. Coffee was Uganda's major export, and Uganda depended on the West to provide a market for it. Amin and his cohorts would have been seriously affected by a coffee boycott. The West was in a position to influence events in Uganda through economic intimidation. If the United States took a strong stand and boycotted Ugandan coffee, the author asserts, other nations would have been encouraged to follow suit. The West's large economic power, maintains the author, should have been against Idi Amin, not in support of him. Ullman was a member of the editorial board of the New York Times *and a former professor of International Affairs at Princeton University.*

By the time this journal is in its readers' hands, the American Congress may have been called upon to decide whether

Richard H. Ullman, "Human Rights and Economic Power: The United States Versus Idi Amin," *Foreign Affairs*, April 1978, vol. 56, no. 3, pp. 529–534, 536–537, 540, 543. Reprinted by permission of FOREIGN AFFAIRS. Copyright © 1978 by the Council on Foreign Relations, Inc. www.foreignaffairs.com.

Uganda's coffee should be barred from entering the United States. Its decision will hold great importance for Uganda, for the United States, and for the international system. At stake will be the issue of whether or not the richest and most powerful of sovereign states is justified in using its economic power unilaterally to force the government of a smaller and weaker state to alter the way it treats its own subjects. . . .

In any contemporary lexicon of horror, Uganda is synonymous with state-become-slaughterhouse. The most conservative estimates by informed observers hold that President Idi Amin Dada and the terror squads operating under his loose direction have killed 100,000 Ugandans in the seven years he has held power. Some estimates run as high as 300,000. Many victims have been guilty of nothing more than catching the eye of the killer—a shopkeeper with coveted goods, a Christian in a Muslim village, a civil servant who questions a command, a judge with foreign friends.

Other governments, in Africa and elsewhere, rule by terror and reward opposition by death. Equatorial Guinea and Cambodia would belong on any list, and there are more. But the scale of official murder in Uganda, its ferocious brutality, and its terrible capriciousness all place Idi Amin's Uganda in a category of its own in which the nearest analogues may be Hitler's Germany or Stalin's Russia. Just as South Africa is unique—an entire system of political and social repression resting on racial distinctions—so Uganda is also. Each, for different reasons, deserves international condemnation.

Thus far, however, Uganda has escaped the kind of censure exemplified by the U.N. Security Council's vote last November [1977] to impose a mandatory arms embargo on South Africa. The most notable act of international censure came at last summer's conference of Commonwealth heads of government when, in Idi Amin's absence, the meeting passed a resolution deploring human rights violations in Uganda. Previously, in March 1977, the U.N. Human Rights Commission—on which Uganda sits—shelved a proposal that it should conduct an investigation into Ugandan conditions. Early last December the five Nordic governments jointly sponsored a U.N. General Assembly resolution condemning Uganda. Immediately it aroused intense controversy within the U.N.'s 50-member African group, with some members even willing to support it. But the majority urged—and the Nordic sponsors agreed—that in exchange for a commitment that the Human Rights Commission would take up Uganda once again in March 1978, the resolution would not be publicly debated or pressed to a vote.

Non-Censure by African States

Not surprisingly, many Westerners contrast African governments' toleration of Uganda with their denunciation of South Africa. Nearly all African leaders have been vociferous in their condemnation of the white regime in Pretoria while remaining silent regarding the black regime in Kampala. African leaders are, indeed, curiously schizophrenic regarding Amin. Many privately admit to abhorring him, and say that he has disgraced Africa. Yet only a few, such as Tanzania's Julius Nyerere and Zambia's Kenneth Kaunda, have said so publicly. The Commonwealth conference succeeded in condemning Uganda last summer only because the resolution of censure did not mention Amin by name and because it passed by acclamation: no head of government had to put his name to it. . . .

Many African leaders refuse to speak or act against Amin for fear of violating the OAU's cardinal rule against interference in a member state's internal affairs. The use of repressive force to maintain order—or power—in new, fragile states composed of multiple tribal groupings is common. Some leaders undoubtedly feel that even though the scale and the capriciousness of official violence in Uganda goes beyond any rational bounds and is fully deserving of repudiation, any effort to condemn Amin would open the door to a process that ultimately would rebound against themselves. Therefore, perhaps the most important factor determining whether or not African governments will ever join in some sort of collective condemnation or action against Idi Amin's regime will be whether they can persuade themselves, as others are already persuaded, that the slaughter in Uganda is indeed a case apart.

There are a few African leaders who purport to believe that the allegations against Amin—well-documented though they are—are fabrications by white racists designed to discredit all African governments. Throughout Africa Amin enjoys a certain popularity because of his theatrical humiliation of whites. . . .

Black African states can censure Amin, and their doing so would be a gesture of great moral significance. Conceivably, they could use coercive force against him. But armed action would endanger ordinary Ugandans and the citizens of the neighboring countries from which a military campaign would come.

Economic Coercion by the West

It is the West, more than black Africa, that holds the power decisively to affect events in Uganda. The alternative to coercion by arms is economic coercion, and only the West can provide it. . . . Uganda depends on the West to provide a market for the Ugandan coffee crop, and coffee is now the country's only export of any significance. A decade or so ago Uganda exported substantial amounts of both cotton and copper, but under Amin its economy has been thrown into such chaos that cotton growing and copper production have virtually ceased, and in recent years coffee has accounted for more than four-fifths of Uganda's exports. . . . During 1977 Uganda benefited substantially from the rise in world coffee prices brought about by the frosts in Brazil and earned some $750 million for its crop, more than double the figures for 1976. No less than one-third of that coffee comes to the United States. Another fifth goes to the United Kingdom, and other Western countries—notably West Germany, France, Italy, Japan, and the Netherlands—buy virtually all the rest.

Uganda's coffee is grown almost entirely by peasant small-holders, not on plantations. Growers are required to sell their beans to the state marketing board, and are paid, at a price set by the board, in vouchers redeemable only in nearly worthless Ugandan shillings. Sometimes they are not even paid at all. Their crop is simply seized. Thus Amin's regime, and not the growers, receives all the foreign exchange. Amin uses it to pay off loans from Libya and other Arab countries, to buy weapons (mostly from the Soviet Union), and to supply his army, police, and civil service with luxury goods. The latter are particularly important to his hold on power: Amin uses lavish material rewards to purchase loyalty.

Present-day Ugandan farmers harvest coffee berries on a large-scale plantation in western Uganda. Many in the West advocated for sanctions on Uganda's coffee as a means to influence political change against Ugandan president Idi Amin. © Bloomberg/Getty Images.

Thus there is a direct relationship between foreign purchases of Uganda's coffee and Amin's murderous regime. Whether he would fall from power if those purchases ceased is a question impossible to answer. Many knowledgeable persons think that he would. There is no doubt, however, that he and his closest collaborators would feel the impact of a boycott of Uganda's coffee, and feel it hard.

Who else would feel it? . . . The vast majority of Ugandans, more than 90 percent and including most of the peasant coffee-growers, depend in large measure upon subsistence agriculture for the necessities of life and participate only marginally in the cash economy. An effective boycott of Uganda's coffee would thus seriously curtail the livelihood only of the country's small urban sector, including Amin's army and police.

There is, of course, the risk that a boycott—especially one that was only partial—would misfire, and merely cause Amin to rule with greater brutality. Even an effective boycott might only induce him to hunker down, rally Ugandans to his side, and wait out the siege. That is doubtful, however. Amin might indeed be able to rally some support. But he is scarcely a popular ruler, and he would have to rely entirely upon sticks, rather than upon the mixture of carrots and sticks he now employs. Moreover, he could not threaten to bring down Uganda's economy with him. It already is down. . . .

Cutting Off US Trade to Uganda

The certainty that the Amin regime would be hurt by a boycott, and the considerable chance that he might even fall from power, has motivated Democratic Congressman Don J. Pease of Ohio, supported by 75 colleagues, to introduce legislation to cut off all American trade with Uganda. They are also sponsoring an alternate, less sweeping bill that would bar Ugandan coffee from entering this country.

Pease would, of course, prefer international action. . . . But he recognizes that, at least for the present, the chances of securing the required international consensus are nonexistent. Even if the U.N. Human Rights Commission should agree to investigate Ugandan atrocities, its inquiry would be likely, at best, to give rise to a General Assembly motion of censure, but not to punitive action. Pease therefore favors a unilateral boycott by the United States, as Uganda's largest export market and supplier of foreign exchange. If an American lead were followed by the United Kingdom, where there is perhaps even a greater awareness and abhorrence of Amin, and by only one or two other Western countries, the impact would likely be large. Even if no other Western government were to follow—and there is no sign that any contemplates doing so—a strong American lead might well stimulate consumer boycotts elsewhere. In any case, denial only of the American market would crimp Uganda's foreign exchange supply. Even that might be enough to precipitate defections from the ranks of Amin's lieutenants. . . .

American policymakers are . . . well aware of the difficulty, in practice, of distinguishing between "economic" and "political" causes and effects. They find it convenient to maintain the rhetorical distinction, however, because of a view that, on balance, American interests are better served in a world in which there is a strong presumption against the overtly political use of economic instruments. Moreover, maintaining the distinction makes it possible to avoid some hard decisions. If unilateral (or Western) economic measures to bring down Amin are ruled out, the peculiar advantage that the United States possesses by virtue of its economic size is neutralized, and the issue of what to do about Amin becomes one of organizing a moral consensus against him. The United States thus becomes only one state among many, and the decision is passed squarely back to Amin's peers, the leaders of other African states. . . .

Undeniably, this is a posture that makes life easier for an American Administration for which, after all, events in Uganda— even if Americans are involved—can never be of continuing central importance. And it is one that carries no risk that the

United States (or a Western coalition) will be labeled as an oppressor of a weak, black Third World state. Even African leaders who privately wish for Amin's downfall might be reluctant to see such an outcome brought about as a result of direct American economic pressure. The precedent might seem too dangerous: in other circumstances they themselves might be Washington's chosen targets. . . .

Taking Action: Separating Economics from Politics

If Congress mandates a boycott of Uganda's coffee by American importers . . . it should do so with a clear awareness of the larger implications of that action. It would indicate, of course, that the U.S. government is prepared to say that there are boundaries of decency beyond which other governments must not pass in their treatment of their own citizens, and that it will suspend official American assistance to those governments. . . .

In the case of Uganda today, the rules of the system, which separate the "economic" from the "political," work entirely to support the brutal regime of Idi Amin. It is, therefore, incumbent upon others who benefit from the normal working of that system—large states and small ones alike—to take action to assure that it no longer provides Amin with the instruments by which he maintains his grasp on power. If possible, that action should be collective. Its impact, not to speak of its international legitimacy, would be much enhanced. But if efforts to bring about collective action by the international community should fail, the United States—and those other major purchasers of Uganda's crucial coffee crop that elect to follow—should take steps to wield the West's large economic power against, rather than in support of, Idi Amin.

The Massacres in Uganda in the 1980s Were Committed Largely by the Government and Its Agencies

Sabiiti Mutengesa

In the following viewpoint, researcher Sabiiti Mutengesa asserts that the widespread, systematic massacres that took place in Uganda in the early 1980s were largely state-inspired genocide. Regions and groups viewed by the regime of President Milton Obote as a political threat suffered the most. The structural crises and societal pressures that plagued Uganda and led to the elimination of entire groups of people, argues the author, resulted from the fact that colonial and post-independence authorities did not integrate the diverse peoples of Uganda. They should have recognized that the different groups needed to be united and accept each other as citizens of the same country, all of whom share a common destiny. There should not have been a "north-south divide." Mutengesa is a former Uganda People's Defense Force (UPDF) officer. He was also a research associate with the Department of War Studies at King's College London.

The very process of the creation of Uganda—initially as a colony and after 1962 as an independent country—laid the ground for much of the debilitating violence that has come to characterize it; a country whose inhabitants' only known tool is a hammer, and for whom every problem has come to resemble a nail.

Throughout her history, Uganda has borne structural crises and societal pressures that would normally have been transitory, but which by not being either properly anticipated or effectively managed have turned into a recurrent malaise and a precondition for authorities and local warlords to eliminate entire groups. Several factors have played a contributory role but I single out the failure by both colonial and post-independence authorities to translate what was originally a mere geographical expression into a united and peaceful people.

Central to this is the integration crisis, namely the failure to socialize the different ethno-racial groups into accepting each other as citizens of one country with a common destiny. The integration deficit derives from several sources, including the pattern of economic and social development that favored the largely Bantu south at the expense of the north, resulting in what is commonly called the "north-south divide." This involved turning the north of the country into a labor reserve for plantation agriculture located in the south and actively discouraging the development of commercial agriculture in the north. Schools and colleges were concentrated in the south of the country, pushing the northern residents further into unskilled employment, with the south providing most of the civil servants, clerks and bureaucrats. The colonial authorities passed legal enactments that established tribally oriented local government units that fostered [according to author F.G. Burke] "a sense of district nationalism and separatism that in many cases did not exist prior to the arrival of the British." Furthermore, the colonial authorities propounded the "martial tribes thesis" to justify the recruitment of members of the armed forces exclusively from the north, a policy that was further pursued by most of the post-independence government.

With this trend of favoring the south in education, commerce and administration of the colony and relegating the north to unskilled labor and the armed forces, there emerged a sense of superiority amongst the inhabitants of the south and centre who tended to refer to the non-Bantu population of the north as non-humans or beasts. . . .

Even the country's name, derived from the Buganda kingdom based in the south, privileged one ethnic group. As one scholar [Samwiri Lwanga-Lunyiigo] would remark, such are the circumstances that would yield "the enthusiasm with which the destruction of [life and] property was undertaken in the Luwero Triangle"; further adding that the brutality was in many ways "a logical conclusion to colonial economic policies: the two zones were evening up the score."

The Military

Economic policies had their counterpart in practices of military formation. Between them, the two sowed the seeds of a possible genocide. The military in Uganda, like similar forces in other colonies, was originally crafted as a custodian of the interests of the colonizing power. . . .

Colonial recruitment emphasized selective preference for the Luo, Sudanic and Nilohamitic sections of the population. Of the 161 officers in the Uganda Army, 141 (88%) were from those groups. In 1969, although the population of the north constituted a mere 19% of the national total, 61% of the military were from that part of the country. [As written by Amii Omara-Otunnu] it was important to the British to ensure that the militaries were, where possible, "an entirely alien mercenary element who did not have any sentimental attachment to Uganda and could be trusted to be brutal without any reserve or compunction.". . .

The first independence regime was led by Milton Obote, whose Uganda People's Congress (UPC) was primarily a vehicle for containing the Baganda's ambitions for political supremacy. Obote, a Langi from the center-north, duly abolished the Buganda monarchy. He was overthrown, not by his Baganda adversaries, but by another northerner, General Idi Amin, who became a parody of an incompetent and brutal dictator. Amin was overthrown in 1979 by a Tanzanian-led invasion, with the Uganda National Liberation Army (UNLA) as its local protégé, drawn chiefly from Obote's followers from the Langi and Acholi. At this stage the country was an economic wreck and deeply divided—problems that the December 1980 elections did nothing to resolve. . . . The elections were a hastily contrived contest between four political parties, namely the Uganda People's Congress (UPC), the Democratic Party (DP), the Conservative Party (CP) and the Uganda Patriotic Movement (UPM). They returned Milton Obote to power.

The massacres occurred in the context of bungled counterinsurgency operations by government forces in the centrally located Buganda region and in the West Nile region in the northwest at the border with the Sudan and then Zaire. The insurgency in the Buganda region was sparked by Milton Obote's return to power, and worse still, doing so through what was widely acknowledged as a fraudulent election. The West Nile insurgency was launched by military elements of the deposed regime of Idi Amin, primarily as a counterattack against the new government, but partly as a consequence of the retributive violence meted out on the population of the region by the Nilotic sections of the UNLA.

Obote's Persecution of the Baganda

The victims of Obote's genocidal massacres fall into three main categories: the Baganda, the "Banyarwanda" and the Sudanic peoples of West Nile.

Following Obote's fraudulent return to power in 1980, it did not require a lot of effort to prod the population of the Buganda heartland to translate their longstanding and deep-seated abhorrence for the man and his party into open rebellion. The UPC sprang onto the political scene as a party to contain Buganda and, as party leader, Obote had done his best to live up to that mission. . . .

In a 12 August 1980 secret memo, he laid out a UPC strategy of conduct before, during and after elections, urging party adherents to remember ". . . how much the Baganda hate me personally," further proposing that "the Baganda especially should be intimidated" for "There was no way their cooperation can be solicited," and further stating how he was ". . . at pains to propose that if necessary leaders of other parties should be eliminated." . . .

Therefore, with Obote's hair trigger readiness to mete out anguish on the populace of Uganda's heartland; or to put it in his own words of 20 years before, "to crush Buganda," . . . it was just a matter of the slightest excuse possible. To provide this excuse, but more so, to skillfully harness the longstanding antipathy for Obote in Buganda, Yoweri Museveni, in command of the National Resistance Army [NRA], set up base in the Luwero Triangle, while other groups like the short-lived Uganda Freedom Movement (UFM) and the Federal Democratic Movement (Fedemo) established themselves in other parts of Buganda especially in the vicinity of the capital, Kampala.

As expected—and one could say, as calculated by the insurgents—Obote's response outdid the most brutal moments of Idi Amin's hellish era. As [African historian] Abdu Kasozi observes, Amin's reign was permanently characterized by violence which "was like a tide, peaking and subsiding at certain periods. Whenever there was a political crisis in the ranks of the regime itself, or when an attempt was made to dislodge the dictator, violence intensified. But in the second Obote period, violence was always at high tide."

In January 1983, Obote launched "Operation Bonanza," a scorched earth campaign, during which the UNLA destroyed small towns, villages, and farms and killed or displaced hundreds of thousands of civilians. By 1984, no significant headway had been registered against the NRA who still maintained strong support among local civilians. Frustrated by its inability to defeat the NRA, the government forces exacted further reprisals against the population, mainly the Baganda, Banyarwanda and

Ankole pastoralists by way of large-scale murder, mass starvation, looting and dislocation of whole communities. . . .

Two More Targets of Government Persecution

In September 1982, the government opened another chapter of ethnic persecution, targeting what the regime collectively lumped up as the "Banyarwanda," affecting at least 100,000 people, mainly in the south of the country. . . .

By subjecting the "Banyarwanda" to persecution the government was on one hand aiming to punish the Bantu groups that were not supportive of the ruling UPC, and to discourage them from supporting the Museveni led insurgency, and on the other, partly actualizing a scheme started in the late 1960s of expelling from Uganda the predominantly Roman Catholic Banyarwanda because of the political cost they placed on the UPC by supporting the DP. . . .

At least 80,000 people were evicted from their homes, half of them finding their way across the border into Rwanda and the other half relocating to UNHCR [United Nations High Commissioner of Refugees] refugee camps in Mbarara.

The Sudanic community of West Nile was the other target. By May 1979, the Tanzanian army and UNLA had "liberated" much of the country save for the West Nile region, Idi Amin's ethnic base. Around this time, the President, Yusuf Lule, was approached by the commander of the Armed Forces, Tito Okello, and the Chief of Staff, David Oyite-Ojok, requesting for permission to "punish the people of West Nile for their misdeeds." The two officers from Acholi and Lango respectively wished to advance on West Nile and take revenge on the Kakwa, Lugbara and Madi for the thousands of their kin murdered by the Amin regime.

Lule turned down the Ojok/Okello request and accordingly instructed the TPDF [Tanzania People's Defence Force] Commander Gen. Msuguri to ensure that the Acholi and Langi contingent of the liberation forces were denied access to the West

Nile region. The Tanzanian commander managed to keep those two groups out of West Nile until he was transferred from the region in 1980 following the deposition of the second post Amin President, Godfrey Binaisa. The replacement of Tanzanian forces by UNLA battalions and militia from Kitgum and Apac areas of Acholi and Lango, respectively, marked the beginning of the systematic devastation of West Nile region and genocidal massacre of the local people. In the months that followed the withdrawal of the TPDF from West Nile, regular Army reinforcements and hordes of the Nilotic militias and volunteers poured into West Nile, this at a time when former Amin soldiers had launched a guerila campaign from across the border in then Zaire.

For every incursion the guerrillas launched, the UNLA set out to massacre the local populace by locking them up in their huts and setting them on fire; this, in addition to looting any movable articles, destroying food stores and desecrating places of worship and burial grounds. . . .

Within a short time, approximately 500,000 residents of West Nile (about 80% of the population of the region) had fled into exile. According to the Minority Rights Group, up to 30,000 people may have been killed by the government forces. . . .

Perpetrators of Genocidal Killing: The State

The main perpetrator of the violence was the state and its agencies, specifically the military, paramilitary organizations, the civil intelligence organizations, specifically the National Security Agency (NASA), local and national officials of the ruling UPC and members of the party's Youth Wing. . . .

The secret police, the National Security Agency (NASA), like its predecessors, the General Service Unit (GSU) of Obote I and Idi Amin's State Research Bureau (SRB) operated above the little that was left of the law and were manned by individuals whose "powers sometimes exceeded their talents." . . .

Party functionaries at all levels, from constituency through parish and village and ordinary party members all over the country, collaborated with the military and the spy agency. There are innumerable instances in which even local administration officials and civil servants, who were generally required to be members of the ruling party, participated in human rights abuses and massacres, with some running private prisons in their homes. . . .

Outlook for the Future

The episodes of genocidal killing in Uganda in the period under examination, namely from 1980-85, came to an end when the Obote regime fell apart under the strains of its own internal contradictions. Whether that brought to an end the structural vulnerability of Uganda to future episodes of genocidal violence is a different question. The answer is not optimistic. . . .

At the national level, Uganda is still a divided and underdeveloped society whose multi-ethnic character will, for years to come, continue to tempt the country's office-seeking political elites to manipulate the otherwise neutral social diversity for personal ends, especially in light of the continuing low level of institutionalization of political participation. The persistent use of military force as the principal arbiter in political contests in this short-fused polity remains a risk factor for mass murder. As Helen Fein posits, "Perpetrators of genocide are often repeat offenders, because elites and security forces may become habituated to mass killing as a strategic response to challenges to state security and also because targeted groups are never destroyed in the entirety." The 1980s may have seen the country stepping back from the brink, but old habits die hard. Much of the same reality that spawned the sad events of the period being discussed still [remain]. As such it may not be imprudent to nominate Uganda for inclusion on the list of countries on which genocide watchers should vigilantly keep tabs.

The Unacknowledged Truths About Persecution and Genocide in Museveni's Uganda

Milton Obote

In the following viewpoint, former Ugandan leader Milton Obote argues that under President Yoweri Museveni, Uganda is not what the international community, media, and human rights organizations say it is. Contrary to their claims, the country is not much improved nor is it rapidly recovering from past agonies. It is a police state where wars and genocide continue. Thanks to a law that prohibits criticism of its shortcomings or crimes, Museveni's National Resistance Army (NRA) has free reign to terrorize and commit other atrocities. The refusal of the international media and human rights organizations to recognize and react to what is happening in Uganda makes it possible for Museveni to do as he wishes with the lives of the Ugandan people. Obote is a former prime minister and president of Uganda. He became the leader of Uganda after its independence in 1962 and again in 1980. His government faced accusations of corruption and violations of human rights.

In 1971, there was a military coup in Uganda. The International Media called Idi Amin, the leader of the coup, "a gentle and

Milton Obote, "Introduction," Notes on the Concealment of Genocide in Uganda, April 1990. Copyright © 1990 by the Uganda People's Congress. All rights reserved. Reproduced by permission.

harmless giant" for about two years, when, in fact, Amin's reign of murder and terror began on the first day of the coup. The international community and the Human Rights Organization took the cue from the media and, with the exception of Tanzania and Zambia, also saw nothing wrong with Amin's murder and terror. Amin's crimes were therefore effectively concealed for two years. Today, Uganda, under [Yoweri] Museveni's militarist regime, has had a state of genocide since 1986. However, Africa and the rest of the world speak a language which Ugandans, who have been and are in the throes of massacres, find it difficult to accept as human language; the language which cleanses Museveni and his militarist regime. . . .

On 28th February, 1990, an academic from Oxford University and I exchanged views on some agonizing and distressing events which have been and are still the lot of Ugandans as well as on the attitude of the international community, media and the Human Rights Organizations. During our conversation, I learned of the International Symposium on Uganda due in May 1990, at Queen's University, Ontario, Canada. . . .

It is to be hoped that the organizers of the Symposium will succeed in their aim: "The Search for Peace in Uganda" and that they would be able to confirm or reject to quote the Prospectus, "the myth that with the departure of Idi Amin and Milton Obote everything in Uganda is now fine". The organizers have an up-hill task: Africa and the entire International Community, since January 1986, have been saturated with propaganda, biased reportage, and down-right disregard of the facts of the situation in Museveni's militarist Uganda. The International Media and Human Rights Organizations such as Amnesty International, Minority Rights Group and International Alert have painted and continue to paint Museveni and his regime in glowing colors that to them there is no myth. According to them, Uganda, under Museveni, is rapidly recovering from the agonies of the past and there is much improvement.

The True State of Affairs Under Museveni

These Notes present the opposite view that Uganda, under Museveni's regime, is a Police State where:

- Genocide has been and still reigns even as I write;

- Entire villages have been and continue to be destroyed by soldiers of the regime as legitimate and proper action against "rebels";

- Foodstuffs in the fields and in granaries in the so-called "war-zones" have been and continue to be uprooted, burnt or destroyed allegedly to deny succor to "rebels";

- Water wells and boreholes in the "war-zones" have been either poisoned or dismantled;

- The entire livestock in several Districts have been looted by the National Resistance Army (NRA), the soldiery of the Museveni regime;

- In the Districts of Gulu, Kitgum, Lira, Soroti, Kumi, a large part of Tororo and now Kasese (population 2.8 million 1979 census) where the NRA soldiers have wrought their greatest havoc, those not massacred, arrested or detained are forced by the soldiers to go to Concentration Camps where many die on various accounts of torture, and from lack of food, water, medication and protection against inclement weather;

- Women in the Concentration camps and in the "war-zones" are at the mercy of the NRA soldiery to abuse as they fancy;

- Soldiers known to be infected with contagious diseases including the deadly HIV are posted to these Concentration camps where they are free to mix and abuse the female inmates. The Concentration camps are in fact cauldrons of genocide where the vulnerable groups (the children, pregnant women and the elderly) are taken to die. . . .

During his first presidency of Uganda, Milton Obote (right) greets the president of Tanzania, Julius Nyerere (left), at Entebbe Airport. Obote argues that his successor, President Yoweri Museveni, allows human rights violations in Uganda. © AP Images.

The Supremacy of the NRA

Museveni has promulgated a law which prohibits not only the pointing out of the shortcomings of or crimes committed by the NRA but also the publication, in whatever form, of the identity or existence of any NRA regiment in any particular area. To dare to point out any shortcoming or crimes of the NRA is to "criticize the NRA" and that in itself is a serious and greater crime than, say, if the NRA had buried people alive or herded them in houses and then burnt the houses, which genocidal practices are quite common in the so-called war zones. The walls of protection which the international media and Human Rights Organizations have erected to protect the regime are such that Museveni, like the mythical James Bond, is thereby licensed to kill and to do whatever he likes with the lives of the citizens of Uganda.

Chapter three of the Constitution of Uganda, has provisions for the "Protection of Fundamental Rights and Freedoms of the Individual". Although he has not suspended this Chapter, Museveni rules as if the provisions of the chapter do not exist and his regime and army have no obligations whatsoever to observe or attempt to observe those provisions. War of aggression is Museveni's chosen method of gross violations of human rights. Under cover of war which he himself instigated, the NRA has massacred Ugandans on a megascale. Under cover of wars, political activities have been banned and comments on the deeds of the NRA are not permitted. In an interview with the BBC [British Broadcasting Corporation] in July 1989, Museveni said: "unfortunately for the BBC the war has ended, so you will not have much to report—it is ended". Yet in the month of February, this year [1990], his own Propaganda Newspaper, *New Vision*, edited by his friend and accomplice William Pike, was reporting the forceful uprooting of 80,000 people from their homes in Kasese District in the far West to concentration camps in order to leave the villages free for artillery bombardment and strafing and thereby destroy homes and foodstuff allegedly to deny succor to rebels. . . .

The fiendishly cruel massacres in the so-called war zones continue unquestionably, despite propaganda to the contrary, to be the main characteristic of Museveni's rule. The massacres and the expanding wars are not freely discussed in any forum in Uganda. . . .

Museveni's Wars

In Uganda of today, it is a treasonable act to exercise the constitutionally guaranteed freedom of conscience, of expression and of assembly and association. What Museveni fully guarantees and rewards handsomely is servile flattery and praises (sychophancy), of his greatness, alleged intrepidity, invincibility and as the only person alive who has all the answers to all the problems (some of them created by him) which afflict Uganda. Thus his wars for all intents and purposes are wars to banish freedom of thought in every brain and home throughout Uganda; and wherever and to whoever submission is humiliation beneath the dignity of a citizen, scorched-earth retribution and massacres are brought into play. . . .

Museveni's determination to consolidate his Police State is clearly observable in the origins and the prosecution of his wars against citizens of Uganda. The current wars in Acholi, Lango and Teso, and North Bukedi are all extensions of Museveni's war in Luwero. The objective origin and the extent and nature of the force used in each case are the same; only rationalization for the purposes of tactics, as publicly stated, have differed.

The perceived wisdom is that Museveni and his NRA were, during the Luwero war, disciplined democrats who had taken up arms against a government they believed was illegitimate. The devastation and atrocities by the NRA in Luwero and later in the North and East show that the perceived wisdom missed the essence of Museveni's wars by a very wide margin: The subjugation of Uganda through extreme terror and violence in order to create a situation of total docility by the people to his will and whims. Through a combination of terror, violence and dissemblance, Museveni created such a situation in Luwero . . . but Luwero was a very narrow base—under 600,000 people (1979 census). Since January 1986, Museveni has been working to expand that base; thus the saturated dissembling propaganda in the "South" and outside Uganda about peace having returned to Uganda while at the same time wars rage in the North and East to expand areas of docility. There can be no doubt that after the subjugation of the North and East, the war of subjugation will be launched in the "South". There are already signs to that effect. . . .

The people of Uganda started their struggle in 1986 against a rapacious, oppressive and massacring regime led by a demented man. They did so in their various localities. Museveni's pet and mocking song is that the uprisings had no cause! Defense against or opposition to these massacres are, to him, not valid. He has

Yoweri Museveni: No Longer a Man of the People

"[Yoweri Museveni's] world outlook has changed," said Augustine Ruzindana, a member of parliament and a fellow survivor of the failed attack on Mbarara in 1972. "There is no doubt that his style of life has changed. He was an ascetic person, very highly disciplined. I think if you discussed something with him and agreed on it, you could rely on that. Now all these things have changed. He likes pomp. I think he likes power for the sake of it. He likes luxury now. He likes money. He has introduced an authoritarianism that was not there. I think that now it's not that he dislikes people who disagree with him. He actually hates them."...

In the 1990s, [US] President Bill Clinton had hailed Museveni as one of a "new breed" of African leaders, but with each egregious scandal, the future was looking more like the past. At press conferences, Museveni sat in a raised white chair, beneath a large portrait of his own face, and hectored the "rumor-mongering" media. "Stop heckling us," he said. "You don't know about the problem of corruption." A satirical play showing in Kampala dramatized the extent to which the president seemed to have fallen out of touch with public opinion. At the end of the production, the playwright, who was also the lead actor, carted out a series of three papier-mâché busts of Museveni, intended to depict how the president had changed over time. One bust had two ears; the second was missing an ear; the third had no ears at all.

Andrew Rice, The Teeth May Smile but the Heart Does Not Forget: Murder and Memory in Uganda. *New York: Metropolitan Books, 2009, pp. 289–290.*

had the advantage because the uprisings were not organized and started simultaneously without prior preparations and were not coordinated. Be that as it may, the point I emphasize here is that the people of Uganda in the North and East—millions of them—

rose against being massacred but the rest of the world has shown an excessive zeal to side with the megaslaughterer, and to underplay the scale of his atrocities. . . .

A Need to Face the Facts

Genocide in Museveni's Uganda is fact. Wars in a very large part of Uganda many times the size of Luwero are facts. Uprising by the people in those war zones to defend lives and property against the massacring NRA soldiery is fact. The abject destitution of the undead is fact. Herding people in houses and setting the houses ablaze by the NRA is fact. Surrounding villages or homesteads and massacring the populace therein by the NRA is fact. Destruction of foodstuff in whole villages to starve the people to death is fact. Poisoning water sources or dismantling the same is fact. Concentration Camps where many, particularly children, die daily and the women inmates are abused in the presence of their relatives or husbands by the NRA soldiery— even those known to have HIV—are facts. Total destruction of the economic structures and means of livelihood in the war zones is fact. That the International Community has not reacted to these facts and others is an enigma. Ugandans are alone in a World where there is much talk about human rights.

The gravity of the situation is strenuously concealed both by the regime and its Revellers [celebrants]. Organizations such as International Alert and Minority Rights Group would appear to want that the regime should "finish off the dirty work" quickly. There is no peace in Museveni's Uganda and there shall be no peace so long as Museveni's regime lasts. The genocide in the North and East will not stop there, new killing fields will be found. The objective of the regime is total docility in all parts of Uganda. . . .

There cannot be any nationalist compromise on the grave matters of ridding Uganda of genocide and a rapacious Police State.

The Causes and Consequences of the War in Northern Uganda Are Many-Sided and Interconnected

Ogenga Otunnu

In the following viewpoint, history professor Ogenga Otunnu recounts occurrences in colonial and post-independence Uganda that he maintains laid a foundation for present-day conflicts there, especially in the northern area known as Acholiland. Colonial economic policies and governmental "divide and rule" policies, for example, helped undermine the legitimacy of the state; delayed the development of a Ugandan nationalism; and created ethnic, religious, and regional divisions that resulted in instability and political violence. The postcolonial regime inherited a fractured state, made worse by the actions of Milton Obote's administration. The war in Acholiland, says the author, became an extension of the post-independence regional and international power struggles and evolved into a full-blown crisis with humanitarian, political, economic, and social dimensions. Otunnu is a professor in DePaul University's Department of History and has published extensively on forced migration, genocide, and nationalism in Africa.

The roots of the current [2002] war between the government of Uganda and the Lord's Resistance Army (LRA) in Acholiland [the northern Uganda districts of Gulu, Kitgum, and Pader] are entwined with the history of conflicts in Uganda and the rise to power of the National Resistance Movement/National Resistance Army (NRM/A). The conflict has persisted because of fragmented and divisive national politics, strategies and tactics adopted by the armed protagonists, and regional and international interests. The harrowing war has claimed many innocent civilian lives, forcefully displaced over 400,000 people and destroyed schools and health centres. In addition, the war has been characterized by widespread and systematic violations of human rights, including rapes, abductions of men, women and children, torture, increased economic decay, and national and regional insecurity. . . .

Conflicts and Fragmentation in Colonial Uganda

Contemporary violent conflicts in the country are directly related to the profound crisis of legitimacy of the state, its institutions and their political incumbents. This crisis, in part, reflects the way the state was constructed through European expansionist violence, manipulation of pre-existing differences, administrative policies of divide and rule and economic policies that further fractured the colonial entity. These policies did not only undermine the faltering legitimacy of the state, but also impeded the emergence of a Ugandan nationalism and generated ethnic, religious and regional divisions that were to contribute in later years to instability and political violence.

One significant divide was along the lines of religious affiliation, which can be traced back to the arrival of Islam, Protestantism and Catholicism in Buganda. These religious groups engaged in a ferocious conflict for dominance, and the Protestant faction emerged victorious after the Imperial British East Africa Company intervened in their favour. Anglicans were to later dominate the top positions in the civil service, and this structural inequality was maintained after the colonial era. Consequently, religious beliefs and political party affiliations were to become entangled.

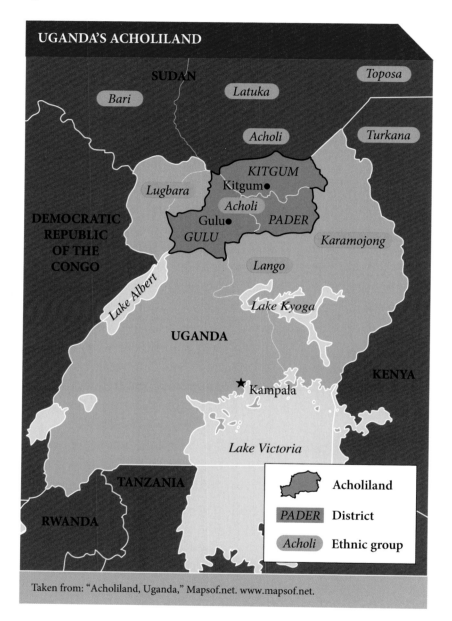

UGANDA'S ACHOLILAND

SUDAN

Toposa

Bari

Latuka

Acholi

Turkana

KITGUM

Lugbara   Kitgum●

Acholi

DEMOCRATIC   Gulu●   PADER
REPUBLIC
OF THE   GULU
CONGO   Karamojong

Lango

Lake Albert   *Lake Kyoga*

UGANDA

KENYA

★ Kampala

Lake Victoria

TANZANIA   Acholiland

PADER   District

RWANDA   Acholi   Ethnic group

Taken from: "Acholiland, Uganda," Mapsof.net. www.mapsof.net.

Conflicts in the colonial state were exacerbated by the partition of the country into economic zones. For example, while a large portion of the territory south of Lake Kyoga was designated as cash crop growing and industrial zones, the territory north of Lake Kyoga was designated as a labour reserve. This partition, which was not dictated by development potentials, led to economic disparities between the south and the north. The fragmentation of the society was compounded by the economic-cum-administrative policy that left the civil service largely in the hands of Baganda and the army largely in the hands of the Acholi and other northern ethnic groups. These policies also widened the gulf between the socio-political south and the socio-political north. This was further sustained by the administrative policy that relied on the Baganda as colonial agents in other parts of the country. The policy of divide and rule, which rested on so-called 'indirect rule', led to widespread anti-Buganda sentiment.

Conflicts and Fragmentation in Post-Independent Uganda

The post-colonial regime inherited a fractured state. Milton Obote responded to this crisis of legitimacy by forming an alliance between his political party, the Uganda People's Congress (UPC) and the Buganda monarchy party (Kabaka Yekka). With this marriage of convenience, Obote became the Executive Prime Minister and Kabaka Mutesa II became the President and Head of State. However, the alliance collapsed over a conflict over land (the 'lost counties') between Bunyoro and Buganda. The 'divorce' led to widespread violence In Buganda. Obote responded by detaining five government ministers from the Bantu region, dismissing the President and Vice President and forcing President Mutesa into exile and suspending the 1962 constitution. The government also imposed a state of emergency in Buganda, occupied Buganda's palace, following the flight of the Kabaka to England, and introduced a republican constitution. Some Bantu-speaking groups perceived this struggle for legitimacy and power as a conflict between the Bantu south and the non-Bantu (Nilotio) north.

These difficulties overlapped with the instability generated in the region by the superpowers' quest for hegemony during the Cold War. These crises were compounded by a conflict between Obote and his army commander, General Idi Amin. In 1971, Amin seized power. Immediately after he came to power, Amin ordered Acholi and Langi soldiers, who constituted the backbone of the army, to surrender their arms. The overwhelming majority of them did so. However, many were subsequently killed. The government extended its conflict with the Acholi and Langi by arresting, detaining and killing highly educated and influential members of the ethnic groups. Over time, Amin began to target people he perceived as disloyal from other parts of the country. To protect the regime which lacked political legitimacy in the country, Amin recruited new soldiers into the national army from West Nile. In addition, he appointed prominent Bantu to important positions in his government. The regime however largely maintained the dominance of southerners in the civil service and commerce, while the northerners largely controlled the government and army.

In April 1979, the exiled rebels, who were overwhelmingly from Acholi and Langi, assisted by the Tanzanian army and Yoweri Museveni's Front for National Salvation (FRONASA), overthrew the Amin regime. Yusuf Lule assumed power. However, ideological and ethnic conflicts within the Uganda National Liberation Front (UNLF) and the national army led to the collapse of the Lule administration within months. Godfrey Binaisa took over, but was himself deposed in May 1980 by Paulo Muwanga and his deputy Yoweri Museveni.

The new administration organized general elections in December 1980, which were won by Milton Obote and his Uganda People's Congress. But widespread irregularities and political violence undermined the legitimacy of the elections. The main challenger, the Democratic Party (DP), rejected Obote's victory. Museveni also rejected the results. Thereafter, a number of armed groups, including Lule's Uganda Freedom Fighters, Museveni's Popular Resistance Army [later they were to merge to form the National Resistance Movement/Army (NRM/A)], and

Dr Andrew Kayira's Uganda Freedom Movement/Army (UFM/A) declared war against the Obote government. In West Nile, Brigadier Moses Ali's Uganda National Rescue Front (UNRF) and General Lumago's Former Uganda National Army (FUNA) also engaged the army and the UPC in bitter armed opposition.

Fighting was particularly intense in the Luwero Triangle, where the mostly Baganda population was targeted for their perceived support of rebel groups. Many innocent civilians were tortured and murdered by the UNLA [Uganda National Liberation Army]. Although the UNLA was a national and multi-ethnic army, the NRM/A held the Acholi exclusively responsible for the atrocities committed, and this disputed perception was to shape subsequent attitudes toward the conflict.

In July 1985, conflict between some Langi and Acholi soldiers led to the overthrow of the Obote regime. The coup, which brought General Tito Okello to power, shattered the military alliance between the Acholi and Langi and escalated ethnic violence. The Okello regime invited all fighting groups and political parties to join the military government. Every armed group and political party, with the exception of the NRA, joined the administration. The NRA, however, engaged the regime in protracted peace negotiations held in Nairobi. In December 1985, the Nairobi Agreement was signed under the chairmanship of President [Daniel arap] Moi of Kenya. However, the Agreement was never implemented and Museveni seized power on the 25th January 1986.

The NRA's seizure of power effectively meant that for the first time, socio-economic, political and military powers were all concentrated in the south. The new administration, which absorbed political and military groups from the south and Moses Ali's UNRF group, engaged in intensive anti-northern propaganda. The administration also discriminated against groups from eastern Uganda and West Nile. This severe alienation and marginalization led to armed conflicts in Teso and West Nile. After much destruction and displacement of the population in Teso, the government negotiated an end to the conflict in the east.

The Conflict in Acholiland

By April 1986, the Acholi had largely come to terms with the NRA victory. The majority of former UNLA soldiers also heeded the appeal made by the government to hand over their arms and demobilize. The response by the Acholi ended the armed engagement in the territory. However, after months of relative calm, anxieties escalated when the NRA began to commit human rights abuses in the name of crushing a nascent rebellion. Over time NRA soldiers plundered the area and committed atrocities, including rape, abductions, confiscation of livestock, killing of unarmed civilians, and the destruction of granaries, schools, hospitals and bore holes escalated. These atrocities in Acholiland were justified by some as revenge for the 'skulls of Luwero'.

Against this background of mistrust and violence, in May 1986 the government ordered all former UNLA soldiers to report to barracks. The order was met with deep suspicion, in part because it was reminiscent of Amin's edict that led to the 1971 massacre of Acholi soldiers. Some ex-UNLA soldiers went into hiding; others fled to Sudan and some decided to take up arms. Soon, these ex-soldiers were joined by a stream of youths fleeing from NRA operations. During this period, the Sudan People's Liberation Army (SPLA), which was perceived by Acholi refugees as an ally of the Museveni government, attacked a refugee camp in southern Sudan. On August 20, 1986, some Acholi refugee combatants, led by Brigadier Odong Latek, attacked the NRA. This armed group, known as the Uganda People's Democratic Army (UPDA), was later joined by the Holy Spirit Mobile Forces/ Movement (HSMF/HSM), Severino Lukoya's Lord's Army, ultimately to be followed by the Lord's Resistance Army (LRA).

The war has lasted for nearly sixteen years because of a number of interrelated factors. To begin with, the war in Acholi has become an extension of regional and international power struggles. On the regional front, Uganda provided military hardware and sanctuary to the SPLA. In retaliation, the Sudan government provided sanctuary and military hardware to the LRA. On the international front, both the Uganda government and the SPLA received military and political support from the US, in the part to curtail the influence of the Islamic government in Khartoum [the capital of Sudan]. Another factor perpetuating the conflict has been that the war has became a lucrative source and cover for clandestine income for high-ranking military and government officials and other profiteers. In addition, the unwillingness of the government and the LRA to genuinely pursue a negotiated settlement has sustained the war. Lastly, atrocities committed by the LRA against unarmed civilians and the unwillingness of the rebel group to accept alternative political views on the conflict have prolonged the war.

The horrific and prolonged consequences of this war have devastated the society—a society that has been reduced to 'displaced camps', where people languish without assistance and

Decades of civil war have forced many northern Ugandans into refugee camps and destroyed much of the culture of the area. © Rick D'Elia/Corbis.

protection. The war has also destroyed the culture and social fabric of the Acholi society. Large numbers of orphans, who fend for themselves, illustrate this tragedy. Furthermore, some children have been abducted by the LRA and forced to torture and kill. Thus, the Rt. Rev. Macleod Baker Ochola II summarized some of the effects the war on Acholiland as follows:

> Violent deaths of our people in the hands of various armed groups; arson perpetrated on mass scale in our land; rape and defilement of our women and girls; abduction of our young people; forced recruitment of our people into rebel ranks; the prevalence of a general atmosphere of fear and disenchantment amongst our people; mass displacement of our people; creation of protected villages which have become breeding grounds for malnutrition and deaths resulting from cholera, measles, and preventable diseases amongst our people; and destruction of our infrastructures and continuous decline in socio-economic growth.

The war has also destabilized other parts of the country and contributed to other regional conflicts in the Great Lakes. The multi-faceted and interrelated causes and consequences of the war should not, therefore, be seen as exclusively an Acholi issue. Nor should the war be treated as merely a humanitarian crisis. It has many dimensions: political, social, economic and humanitarian. As such, durable solutions will need to respond to all of these challenges.

The Abuses of the Lord's Resistance Army Violate the Principles of International Humanitarian Law

Human Rights Watch

In the following viewpoint, a Human Rights Watch report asserts that for more than ten years the Lord's Resistance Army (LRA) blatantly violated the most elementary principles of international humanitarian law. The LRA has devastated northern Uganda—pillaging, looting, burning down houses and schools, displacing and massacring thousands of civilians. It has abducted young children, made them slaves, and forced them to become LRA soldiers and take part in the atrocities being committed by the adults. Those children who do manage to escape often find themselves without homes and not accepted by their communities. The Lord's Resistance Army needs to fulfill its obligations under international humanitarian law—and the Ugandan government and the international community must do more to support these children and protect their rights, the report maintains. Human Rights Watch is a leading independent organization dedicated to protecting the human rights of people worldwide.

In northern Uganda, thousands of children are victims of a vicious cycle of violence, caught between a brutal rebel group

"The Scars of Death: Children Abducted by the Lord's Resistance Army in Uganda," Human Rights Watch, September 1997, pp. 2–3, 48–51, 54, 56, 58–64, 66, 87–88, 95, 100–101. Copyright © 1997 by the Human Rights Watch. All rights reserved. Reproduced by permission.

and the army of the Ugandan government. The rebel Lord's Resistance Army (LRA) is ostensibly dedicated to overthrowing the government of Uganda, but in practice the rebels appear to devote most of their time to attacks on the civilian population: they raid villages, loot stores and homes, burn houses and schools, and rape, mutilate and slaughter civilians unlucky enough to be in their path.

When the rebels move on, they leave behind the bodies of the dead. But after each raid, the rebels take away some of those who remain living. In particular, they take young children, often dragging them away from the dead bodies of their parents and siblings.

The rebels prefer children of fourteen to sixteen, but at times they abduct children as young as eight or nine, boys and girls alike. They tie the children to one another, and force them to carry heavy loads of looted goods as they march them off into the bush. Children who protest or resist are killed. Children who cannot keep up or become tired or ill are killed. Children who attempt to escape are killed. . . .

In effect, children abducted by the Lord's Resistance Army become slaves: their labor, their bodies and their lives are all at the disposal of their rebel captors. . . .

The Children's Plight

In its 1996 report to the U.N. [United Nations] Committee on the Rights of the Child, the Ugandan government affirmed its general commitment "to improve the lives of . . . child soldiers" and its "special concern" for children abducted by rebels. Nonetheless, the Uganda Child Rights NGO [nongovernmental organization] Network (UCRNN) has been critical of the government's response to the crisis in the north, noting that while the Museveni government provided "special services" for children who were caught up in civil wars of the early 1980s (when Museveni's guerrilla army fought the Obote and Okello regimes), "children caught up in the armed rebellion in northern Uganda since 1987 have not received adequate support from the government." According to UCRNN, "no government programmes or resources have been identified" for children abducted by the Lord's Resistance Army. UCRNN has called upon the government to "take concrete measures to address the needs of children caught up in armed conflict" and to "establish adequate responses for the long-term support of these children."

Some of the children who escape from the rebels go immediately home to their villages, and some return to their boarding schools, but many end up staying, for a time, at the trauma centers operated by World Vision or the Gulu Save the Children Organization (GUSCO). Conditions in the centers are poor: too many children in small huts and tents, too few trained counselors, and not enough for the children to do. . . .

But at least the centers feel safe to the children: at the centers, they are surrounded by other children who have gone through similar experiences, and cared for by supportive, non-judgmental adults. This is not always the case outside of the centers: according to [World Vision's] Robby Muhumuza, children who return home sometimes find that other families with young relatives still in captivity are "jealous of those who have returned." Some people also blame the children for rebel atrocities. Those villagers who had themselves suffered at the hands of Lord's Resistance Army rebels are sometimes "antagonistic, labeling the children 'rebels.'" Occasionally, children face physical threats from community members who identify them as perpetrators of atrocities.

For girls, in a culture which regards non-marital sex as "defilement," the difficulties are even greater: reviled for being "rebels," the girls may also find themselves ostracized for having been "wives." They fear "shame, humiliation and rejection by their relatives and possible future husbands." They may suffer "continual taunts from boys and men [who say they are] used products that have lost their taste."

For many children, lack of community acceptance is the least of their troubles. "Many of these children have parents who were

Women displaced from their homes by the Lord's Resistance Army (LRA) wait for food distribution in Lira, Uganda. © AP Images/Peter Busomoke.

killed during their abductions," explains World Vision's Charles Wotman. "Others have families, but they have been displaced, and no one knows where they are." Children without families worry that they will be unable to support themselves. Even those children with supportive homes and communities fear leaving the centers, because of the danger of being re-abducted and killed. . . .

Gross Violation of Humanitarian Law

The human rights abuses of the Lord's Resistance Army shock the conscience, and violate the most elementary principles of international humanitarian law. The LRA's abuses of children's rights are both too numerous and too self-evident to make an exhaustive list of relevant international human rights standards necessary. Most pertinently, however, the LRA's actions violate the provisions of Common Article 3 of the Geneva Conventions of 1949, which lays out the minimum humanitarian rules applicable to internal armed conflicts: . . .

(1) Persons taking no active part in the hostilities, including members of armed forces who have laid down their arms and those placed *hors de combat* by sickness, wounds, detention, or any other cause, shall in all circumstances be treated humanely, without any adverse distinction founded on race, colour, religion or faith, sex, birth or wealth, or any other similar criteria. . . .

Since Common Article 3 of the Geneva Conventions is binding on "each Party to the conflict"—that is, it is binding on both governmental and non-governmental forces—the Lord's Resistance Army currently stands in flagrant violation of international humanitarian law. . . .

The Toll Taken in the North

Abducted children are not the only victims of the conflict in the north. The conflict, which has now persisted for over a decade, has taken the lives of thousands of civilians of all ages. Some have been killed by the rebels during raids; others have been caught in the crossfire between rebels and government soldiers. While at times several weeks go by with few rebel attacks, during other periods, the death toll is astounding: during a single two-week period in July 1996, for instance, violence took the lives of forty soldiers, thirty-two rebels and 225 civilians. Between January 6 and January 10, 1997, 400 civilians were slaughtered during a rebel attack in Kitgum.

Northern Uganda today faces an acute humanitarian crisis. The two northern districts of Gulu and Kitgum, the homeland of the Acholi people, have been hardest hit: relief agencies estimate that over 240,000 people are currently displaced from their homes and villages, while some local officials estimate that the figure is as high as two million displaced people. In Kitgum, nearly half of the displaced people are children, and more than a third of those children have been orphaned by the war.

The infrastructure in Gulu and Kitgum is in a state of collapse. The constant danger of land mines and rebel ambushes has made many of the region's few roads unsafe for travel. Rebel attacks destroyed thousands of homes. Agriculture has come to a standstill in parts of the region, since the insecurity has forced people to flee their homes and abandon their fields.

Education, too, has stopped in many places. The rebels target schools and teachers, and in the last year, in Gulu alone, more than seventy-five schools have been burnt down by the rebels, and 215 teachers have been killed. Many more teachers have been abducted or have fled the region. An estimated 60,000 school-aged children have been displaced. . . .

The Health Crisis

The health care system in the north, always rudimentary, has almost collapsed. Many of those who are wounded in the fighting receive little or no medical attention; as a result, figures giving the number of dead and wounded are almost certainly too low, since many deaths and injuries never come to the attention of the authorities. Rebel raids on clinics and dispensaries have diminished the store of medicines available, and the instability has caused many health workers to flee. This has disrupted most basic non-emergency services, including immunization campaigns. Officially, there are thirty rural health units in Gulu, but as of May 1997, only fourteen remained in operation.

The results are predictable: by almost any health care indicator, Gulu and Kitgum lag far behind other parts of Uganda. At the end of 1995, for instance, the infant mortality rate in Gulu was 172 per thousand live births, compared to eighty per thousand live births in Kampala. Most estimates suggest that the HIV infection rate in the region hovers at around 25 percent of the population. And AIDS deaths compound all of the region's other problems, further straining health care resources, rendering immune-compromised people more vulnerable to other diseases, and leaving still more children orphaned.

The health crisis has been greatly exacerbated by the government policy of encouraging civilians to leave rural areas and move to "protected camps" near Uganda People's Defense Force military installations. The rationale behind the protected camps is straightforward: by concentrating the civilian population in a few well-defined areas, the army hopes both to simplify the task of protecting people from rebel attacks and make it harder for the rebels to find food by raiding villages. But in practice, the protected camps have been, at best, a mixed blessing for the internally displaced people of Gulu and Kitgum: tens of thousands of them thronged to the camps, only to find that virtually no provision had been made for sanitation or sustenance. . . .

Unsurprisingly, limited water, poor sanitary facilities and minimal provision of medical care in the protected camps has led to thousands of deaths each month. Ten of the twenty-four camps in Gulu district are situated in areas with no health care facilities at all, and a recent survey in three of the camps found that 41.9 percent of the children were malnourished. Epidemics of measles, malaria and dysentery kill off many of the weakest in the camps. . . .

According to Paulinus Nyeko of Gulu Human Rights Focus, civilians frequently complain of harassment and human rights abuses by the Ugandan People's Defense Force, including robbery, rape and torture. . . . [The] public relations officer for the UPDF in Gulu confirmed that he was aware of such allegations, and attributed any such incidents to "communication problems" stemming from "ethnic difficulties and language differences."

Why the Conflict Persists

The uneven economic development of north and south and the history of ethnic violence have cast a long shadow over Uganda. For the Acholi people, the legacy of the decades following independence has been one of demoralization and distrust. This climate of hopelessness has provided the rebel Lord's Resistance Army with ideal conditions for sowing discord and terror.

The rebels themselves claim that they will fight until they overthrow the government of [Ugandan president] Yoweri

Museveni. . . . The rebels appear to view Museveni as an illegitimate leader because of his refusal to allow multi-party elections, his alleged strategy of keeping the north poor and under-developed, and his alleged dislike and mistreatment of the Acholi. The rebels still insist that they are obeying the orders of the Holy Spirit, and there can be little doubt that religious rituals, of however eclectic a nature, are important in rebel life. The rebels continue to claim that they must root out "misbehavior" and offenses among the Acholi as part of their effort to overthrow the government and turn Uganda into a "paradise.". . .

While [LRA leader Joseph] Kony's control over the Lord's Resistance Army is near total, a great number—perhaps even a large majority—of the "rebels" are abducted children, rather than adults who voluntarily joined Kony. Terrified and indoctrinated, the children participate in atrocities along with the adults. Although some of the children obey their captors only out of a wholly non-spiritual fear, some of them certainly believe what they are told about the Holy Spirit, and some of them grow to adulthood among the rebels, and cease to imagine having any other identity.

In the end, some of the rebels probably commit atrocities out of the sincere belief that they are obeying the Holy Spirit's orders to eliminate wrongdoers within the Acholi community; some probably participate in atrocities only because they fear being killed if they refuse; some may literally be unable to imagine any other life, and some may be acting solely to increase their personal power and prestige. And some, of course, may act out of a combination of all of those motives.

Needless to say, despite all Lord's Resistance Army claims to be fighting on behalf of the Acholi, and despite whatever popular Acholi support Kony may have had in the late 1980s, it seems overwhelmingly clear that today the Acholi people regard Lord's Resistance Army activities as an unmitigated evil. . . .

Many Acholi see their situation as hopeless: whatever happens, they suffer. "When the government fights the rebels lately,

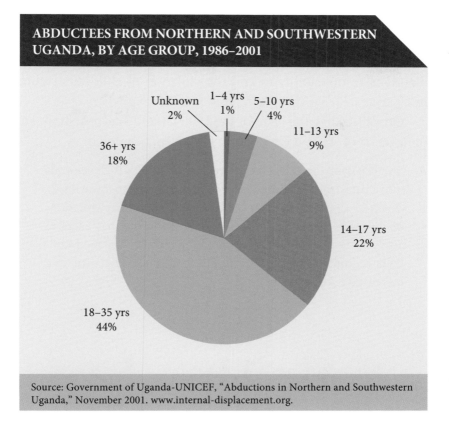

ABDUCTEES FROM NORTHERN AND SOUTHWESTERN
UGANDA, BY AGE GROUP, 1986–2001

Unknown 2%
1–4 yrs 1%
5–10 yrs 4%
11–13 yrs 9%
36+ yrs 18%
14–17 yrs 22%
18–35 yrs 44%

Source: Government of Uganda-UNICEF, "Abductions in Northern and Southwestern Uganda," November 2001. www.internal-displacement.org.

mostly it is local defense units [the militia] being sent to fight, not the regular UPDF soldiers," said Paulinus Nyeko. "Since it is mostly Acholi in the local defense units, and they go to fight Acholi rebels, many of whom are abducted children, what we have now is Acholi fighting Acholi children. If this conflict does not end we will have none of us left.". . .

Although children are far from the only ones who are suffering as a result of the Lord's Resistance Army, it is unquestionably the very young who are suffering the most. . . . Even if the crisis ended tomorrow, the effects of the Lord's Resistance Army's atrocities will haunt Uganda for generations to come.

The Lord's Resistance Army should comply with its obligations under international humanitarian law, and the government of Uganda should take all possible steps to protect the rights of Ugandan children, as required by the Convention on the Rights of the Child. But the international community, too, has a tremendous responsibility to end the violation of children's rights in Uganda.

Graca Machel, the head of the 1996 United Nations Study on the Impact of Armed Conflict on Children, has noted:

> The crisis in the Great Lakes region of Africa is developing into a catastrophic human tragedy. Despite repeated warnings, despite increasing numbers of deaths, despite clear violations of children's rights, the international community has failed to act. . . . The protection and care of children in armed conflicts requires greater political will, continued vigilance, and increased cooperation.

The International Community Must Act to End the Human Rights Catastrophe in Northern Uganda

Olara A. Otunnu

In the following viewpoint, human rights activist Olara A. Otunnu proclaims that what is happening in northern Uganda is not a routine crisis but a "methodical and comprehensive genocide" of an entire society. He chastises the international community for not responding to the dire situation and accuses them of putting political considerations ahead of humanitarian responsibilities. He asserts that the international community must take action to denounce and stop genocide wherever it takes place, no matter what ethnic group the people being destroyed belong to or what their politics are. Otunnu has served as United Nations under-secretary general and special representative for children and armed conflict, chairman of the UN Commission on Human Rights, and vice president of the UN General Assembly.

As we meet here today [November 9, 2005] to focus on the fate of children being destroyed in situations of war, I must draw your attention to the worst place on earth, by far, to be a child today. That place is the northern part of Uganda.

Human rights activist Olara A. Otunnu has strongly advocated for international action against the ongoing genocide in Uganda. © AP Images/Donald Stampfli.

What is going on in northern Uganda is not a routine humanitarian crisis, for which an appropriate response might be the mobilization of humanitarian relief. The human rights catastrophe unfolding in northern Uganda is a methodical and comprehensive genocide. An entire society is being systematically destroyed—physically, culturally, socially, and economically—in full view of the international community. In the sobering words of a missionary priest in the area, "Everything Acholi is dying". I know of no recent or present situation where all the elements that constitute genocide under the Convention on the Prevention and Punishment of the Crime of Genocide (1948) have been brought together in such a comprehensive and chilling manner, as in northern Uganda today.

The situation in northern Uganda is far worse than that of Darfur [Sudan], in terms of its situation, its magnitude, the scope of its diabolical comprehensiveness, and its long-term impact and consequences for the population being destroyed. For example, Darfur is 17 times the geographic size of northern Uganda and 4 times the size of its population, yet northern Uganda has had 2 million displaced persons for 10 years, the same as the number of displaced persons in Darfur today. The situation in Darfur has lasted for 2½ years now; the tragedy in northern Uganda has gone on for 20 years now, with the forced displacement and concentration camps having lasted now for 10 years. I applaud the attention and mobilization being focused by the international community on the abominable situation in Darfur. But what shall I tell the children of northern Uganda when they ask: how come the same international community has turned a blind eye to the genocide in their land?

Political Considerations vs. the Responsibility to Protect

How shall I explain to the perplexed children that those on whom they had counted to defend their human rights have instead become the cheerleaders and chief providers of succour and support for a regime that is presiding over genocide, a regime which celebrates systematic repression, ethnic discrimination and hatred, impunity and corruption, under 20 years of one-party rule, a regime which routinely and chillingly gloats about destroying "those people"—"those people" and their children?. . .

As it happens, last September [2005], world leaders meeting at the special UN [United Nations] summit in New York adopted an important declaration on "Responsibility to Protect." They have made a solemn commitment to act together to protect populations exposed to genocide and grave dangers, when their own government is unable or unwilling to protect them, or, worse, when the state itself is the instrument of a genocidal project. This has been precisely the situation in northern Uganda for twenty years. But for those 20 years, political considerations have trumped "responsibility to protect." And in that calculus, the children and women of northern Uganda have become literally expendable.

The genocide in northern Uganda presents the most burning and immediate test case for the solemn commitment made by world leaders in September. Will the international community on this occasion apply "Responsibility to Protect" objectively, based on the facts and gravity of the situation on the ground, or will action or inaction be determined by 'politics as usual'?

Northern Uganda: A Region and People in Crisis
Witness the following:

- This human rights and humanitarian catastrophe in northern Uganda has been going on, non-stop, for twenty years.
- For over 10 years, a population of almost 2 million people have been herded into concentration camps (some 200 camps in all), having been forcibly removed from their homes and lands by the government. Such *en masse* forced displacement and instrument is reminiscent of similar exercises conducted in apartheid South Africa and Khmer Rouge's Cambodia. Today virtually the entire population of Acoli (95%) is in these concentration camps, in abominable conditions—massively congested with woeful sanitation and rampant with diseases. As one elder summarized it, "People are living like animals."
- According to a recent conservative estimate, 1,000 people die in these camps per week; this means 4,000 lives every month, and about 50,000 deaths every year. This does not include those who have been killed in outright atrocities.
- These camps have the worst and most dramatic infant mortality rates anywhere in the world today.
- Chronic malnutrition is widespread; 41% of children under 5 years have been seriously stunted in their growth.

- Two generations of children have been denied education as a matter of policy, they have been deliberately condemned to a life of darkness and ignorance, deprived of all hope and opportunity. . . .

- For a society which has been so renowned for its deep-rooted and rich culture, values system and family structure, all three have been destroyed under the weight of the conditions systematically imposed in the camps. This loss is colossal; it signals the death of a society and a civilization.

- In the face of relentless cultural and personal humiliations and abuse, suicide, serious depression and alcoholism have become rampant.

- Rape and generalized sexual exploitation, especially by soldiers, have become "entirely normal." In Uganda, HIV/AIDS has become a deliberate weapon of mass destruction. Soldiers who have tested HIV-positive are then especially deployed to the north, with the mission to commit maximum havoc on the local girls and women. Thus from almost zero base, the rates of HIV infection among these rural communities have galloped to dramatic levels. This, even as official propaganda touts Uganda's example the model for the fight against HIV/AIDS!

- The population has been deprived of all means of livelihood; they have been denied access to their lands, while the entire mass of their livestock was forcibly confiscated and simply exported from the north.

- Over the years, thousands of children have been abducted by the LRA [Lord's Resistance Army].

- Some 40,000 children, the so called "night commuters," trek many hours each evening to reach the towns of Gulu and Kitgum (and walk back the same distances in the morning) to avoid abduction by the LRA.

Kitgum: An Example of Terror and Neglect

The scene in Kitgum, the heart of the area experiencing the worst LRA [Lord's Resistance Army] terror and Ugandan government neglect was one of the most profoundly disturbing I have experienced in all my years of humanitarian work. Daylight was fading as we arrived at the village school that doubled as a health post. As the sun set over the hills the first of more than a thousand children, some as young as two or three, accompanied by their mothers, began to shuffle into the grounds to spend the night lying huddled together in rooms and corridors and on the pavement outside. They were just a small proportion of the estimated forty thousand children, so-called "night commuters," who gather every evening at several impromptu "safe" meeting points in local towns and villages. . . . As dawn breaks the children begin their journeys back to their scattered huts and shelters, only to return that same evening.

- The population has been rendered totally vulnerable; they are trapped between the gruesome violence of the LRA and the genocide atrocities; humiliations are being systematically committed by the government. . . .

The Need to Act

The grim facts outlined above are well known in foreign chancelleries, UN agencies, international NGOs [nongovernmental organizations] and human rights organizations. Yet, with a few exceptions, those in a position to raise their voices and to act have instead joined in a conspiracy of silence. This betrayal is all the more painful because it has come from the very governments and organizations they had counted on to mount a vigorous defence of their human rights. We have applauded these

All the children told similar stories of living in continuous fear of attacks on their settlements while being utterly neglected by the Ugandan government and the international community. Some blankets are passed around by NGOs and church groups but there is no food, no medicine, no counseling, no registration, and no journalists—only sadness and lost childhoods. My African colleague was right when he said this was perhaps our "number one forgotten failure."

The next morning I asked my UN [United Nations] colleagues to meet me on the veranda of our guest house. I was angry and still reeling from the desperately sad scenes of the day before. Some of those I was addressing had worked in Uganda for months, even years, but had never bothered to make the daylong journey north. "I hope you all agree we cannot continue like this," I told a group of nodding heads, "We have failed utterly here. You and your organizations have to step up action dramatically and I will do all I can to wake up donors and headquarters." They were rightly embarrassed.

Jan Egeland, A Billion Lives: An Eyewitness Report from the Frontlines of Humanity. *New York: Simon & Schuster, 2008, pp. 202–203.*

governments for making the values of human rights, democracy, good governance and accountability a cornerstone of their international policy, and yet concerning the cynical and consistent negation of these values in Uganda, they have adopted a policy of "We see no evil, we hear no evil".

There is need for a very, very deep soul-searching about what has been going on in Uganda. The Ugandan situation and the response to it—or rather the conspicuous lack of response thereto—raises some very disturbing questions about the discourse and the application of human rights policies by the international community.

Today, from this podium and on this important occasion of the award of the Sydney Peace Prize, I wish to address a most urgent appeal—a *cri de coeur* [cry from the heart]—to the leaders of the western democracies in particular, concerning the genocide in northern Uganda. It is with a heavy and anguished heart that I do so. But I must do so for the sake of the children and in the name of the 2 million people being destroyed in the 200 camps of death [and] humiliation.

We must retrieve the path of a principled application of human rights. There must be one set of human rights for all victims, or we undermine human rights discourse for all victims. When human rights are applied selectively, we reap a whirlwind of cynicism.

We must denounce and stop genocide wherever it occurs, regardless of the ethnicity or political affiliation of the population being destroyed.

For the sake of the children, and the 2 million people in the concentration camps, I appeal to the western democracies to review their continued sponsorship and support for a regime that is orchestrating and presiding over the genocide of its own population.

I wonder if we have learned any lessons from history. When millions of Jews were exterminated during the Holocaust in Europe, we said 'never again,'—but after the fact. When genocide was perpetrated in Rwanda, we said 'never again,'—but again after the fact. When children and women were massacred in Srebrenica, we said 'never again,'—but after it was all over. The genocide unfolding in northern Uganda is happening on our watch, and with our full knowledge. Why is there no action?

The Commission of Inquiry into Violations of Human Rights Failed

Joanna R. Quinn

Ugandan president Yoweri Museveni appointed the Commission of Inquiry into Violations of Human Rights (CIVHR) in 1986. In the following viewpoint, McMaster University student Joanna R. Quinn contends that even though the commission expected to be successful, it was not. There were, says the author, a number of reasons for this. For one, the commission did not get the tools or funds it needed to do its job and achieve its objectives. Another contributing factor was the lack of political will in support of the commission and its work. As a result, it took the commission eight years to finish its report, a time span that proved too long for the report to have an impact or stay in the memories of most Ugandans.

In the aftermath of a period of gross atrocity at the hands of the state, the restoration of the political and social fabric of a country is a pressing need. In the case of Uganda from the mid-1960s forward, this need was particularly real. Almost since the country had gained independence from Britain in 1962, a series of brutal governmental regimes had ransacked the country,

Joanna R. Quinn, "The Politics of Acknowledgement: An Analysis of Uganda's Truth Commission," YCISS Working Paper. Toronto, Ontario: York Centre for International and Security Studies, March 2003, pp. 1–2, 4–6, 20–22. Copyright © 2003 by Joanna R. Quinn. All rights reserved. Reproduced by permission.

and had viciously dealt with its inhabitants. Nearly thirty years of mind-numbing violence, perpetrated under the regimes of Idi Amin and Milton Obote, culminated in a broken society. Where once had stood a capable people, able to provide for themselves on every level, now was found a country whose economic, political, and social systems were seriously fractured.

Under both Obote and Amin, as well as the transitional governments in place between and immediately following these regimes, democracy and the rule of law had been suspended. Instead, beginning in 1962 with Obote's first term in office, and continuing throughout the regimes of Amin and the second regime of Obote (commonly referred to as Obote II), as well as the various transitional governments put in place for short periods of time, a series of brutal crimes was carried out. Often depending on ethnic affiliation and/or societal status, Ugandans were subjected to all manner of abuses, from arbitrary arrest and detention to wholesale slaughter and mass murder. From one regime to the next, different tribal groups were targeted, then tortured and killed. . . .

Hundreds of thousands of people were murdered throughout the period, while the various heads of Ugandan government sought to legitimize their rule and cement their positions of power in any way possible. . . .

When [Yoweri] Museveni seized control of the government in 1986 after nearly fifteen years of bush warfare, he set about rebuilding the shattered nation. He outlined a ten-point programme in which he emphasized democracy, security, national unity, independence, restoring and rehabilitating social services, ending corruption and misuse of power, dealing with the plight of displaced people, pan-African cooperation and pursuing a mixed economy as the basic tenets of his philosophy.

In pursuit of these goals, Museveni established, among other institutions, a truth commission to address the wrongs which had been perpetrated. The role of the Commission of Inquiry into Violations of Human Rights (CIVHR) was to inquire into "the causes and circumstances" surrounding mass murders, arbitrary arrests, the role of law enforcement agents and the state security agencies, and discrimination which occurred between 1962 and January 1986 when Museveni and the NRM [National Resistance Movement] assumed power. It was also meant to suggest ways of preventing such abuses from recurring. The Commission was also expected to determine the role of various state institutions in both perpetrating and hiding gross human rights violations. The government promised that the results and findings of this Commission would be treated seriously. . . .

The Commission of Inquiry into Violations of Human Rights

In 1986, Museveni's government was simply seen as the next in a series of military coups, a military government fighting to hold on to what legitimacy it could. His statements in favour of democracy, therefore, combined with his progressive stance on dealing with Uganda's recent past, were a nice bit of window-dressing. For, as Museveni's initial term in office wore on, it began to seem that he had no genuine intention of supporting the truth commission in any real way. After several months in power, Museveni and the NRM chose to focus on strengthening Uganda's economy, and on rebuilding the military and police force in their quest for "the rule of law." In doing so, it sometimes sacrificed human rights for the greater good of Museveni's own agenda. . . .

The Commission of Inquiry into Violations of Human Rights was appointed on 16 May 1986, three months after Museveni had taken office. The Commission was inaugurated one month later, on 13 June 1986. Until the tabling of the Report on 10 October 1994, the Commission worked to gather evidence and testimony relating to the events of 1962–1986. Thousands of people completed questionnaires with regard to their recollection of particular events, many of which were then investigated in the field. From these, particularly strong and representative cases were chosen to go before the Commission. In all, 608 witnesses appeared before the CIVHR from 11 December 1986 to 07 April 1993. The Commission travelled to virtually every region of the country, holding hearings and collecting testimony in seventeen districts. . . .

The following is an account of one of the Commissioners in describing the testimony and hearings process:

> You know, for us—I speak for myself—to begin with, I didn't know that the crimes that had been committed were that many, and that hideous. It was shocking to me because, okay, I knew that so-and-so was arrested. You knew that people we knew were killed. So you limit your knowledge to those you know, or to those who were reported in the newspaper. But when you open the Commission for the whole country and you see the response, and the crimes in all the areas of the country, it was shocking. It was shocking to me. And everyday, I expected a new story. Everyday, I expected a new kind of crime. The crimes were so—you can imagine—you think maybe that they have been arrested, imprisoned . . . but when they arrested them and assaulted them, there's also forms of torture that you never get to hear . . . the forms of torture he goes through and he kills him. And then the helplessness after these things. And psychological sickness they go through. The death that follows. And the disintegration of the family. If the head of the family is arrested, the whole family seems to sort of, you know, everybody suffers. So to me . . . I feel it really brought me a new dimension of what took place and how society at large suffered.

The Commission of Inquiry into Violations of Human Rights was Museveni's answer to dealing with the legacy of nearly twenty-five years of mass atrocity. Certainly, many of those appointed to share in the task of carrying out the Commission's work were confirmed patriotic human rights supporters who were honoured to have been asked to participate; others were selected because of their strong knowledge of the law. In every case, their appointments were made because of a specified set of knowledge and/or experience that each had. . . . Altogether, there were six: a lawyer, a professor of law, a judge, a professor of history and sometime women's advocate, a writer, and a medical doctor-turned-member of parliament who had been with Museveni since his days in the bush. Any casual observer might rightfully have thought that this combination of personalities and years of experience would be enough to carry the Commission through to a successful conclusion.

Museveni was hasty in appointing the Commission. Its mandate was extremely broad and vague. It included the need to investigate nearly every type of human rights abuse imaginable, all of which had been committed between the time of Independence in 1962 and the beginning of Museveni's term in office. The legislation listed nine wide-ranging categories of violations for consideration, along with a clause demanding that the Commissioners consider "any other matter connected with or incidental to the matters" already mentioned. These included investigation of mass murder; arbitrary arrest, detention and imprisonment; unfair trials; torture; crimes of law enforcement agents; the displacement, expulsion or disappearance of Ugandans; discriminatory treatment; the denial of any human right; the protection of anyone who had perpetrated such crimes; and anything else the Commission deemed necessary. Otherwise, the scope, size, and subject matter for consideration were largely undetermined, as was the manner in which such abuses ought to be dealt with. Neither the fact that these abuses totaled well into the hundreds of thousands, nor were specified, was addressed. Instead, the fledgling group of Commissioners were left to sort out such issues. . . .

Why the CIVHR Did Not Succeed

The Commission of Inquiry into Violations of Human Rights had every hope of succeeding. . . . Among the Commissioners was a collective spirit of honour, of urgency, and of a need to prevent and protect against future human rights abuses.

In spite of all this commitment, the Commission was fraught with difficulties. Eight years and countless hold-ups later, the Commission released its report with a quiet whimper. Even to-day [2003] the Report of the Commission is not widely available within the country, let alone in the rest of the world. . . . On so many levels, the Commission was prevented from doing its job. The constraints it faced were enough to seriously erode what impact it might have had, and to render it impotent as a mechanism of truth-seeking and potentially of justice.

The Report is a strikingly large and imposing document, even in its paper-bound version. The evidence it contains is sickening. It describes and documents cases of brutal abuse, rape, and murder. It apportions blame. It makes exacting recommendations, some of which were accepted. Uganda's new Constitution contains a section on human rights, and the UHRC [Uganda Human Rights Commission] has been up and running now for more than five years. The Ugandan government has now ratified many of the international human rights treaties, and the police service is now under review. Most of the other recommendations have been ignored.

Sadly, the majority of Ugandans know little or nothing about the Report, because they have never seen it. In an attempt to get the news contained in the final Report to the people, a small pamphlet was also produced which summarized the findings of the Commission and was to be widely distributed. Instead, due to lack of funds and a waning interest in all things related to sorting out Uganda's past, this never happened. . . .

The institutional failures of the Commission alone were enough to cause it to be derailed. The CIVHR was simply not invested with the tools it needed to do a thorough job; its capacity both to carry out its duties and to effect change in the greater community was minimal at best. The chronic under-funding endured by the Commission caused disruptions in its work and made external funding a necessity for its completion. This pattern has, in turn, been imprinted on the new Uganda Human

Rights Commission: a legitimate cause for concern regarding the legitimacy of the commitment made by Museveni to the cause of human rights and justice. The result of these and other obstacles faced by the CIVHR was, of course, the eight years that it took to complete the work.

Equally significant, however, was the lack of political will in support of the Commission. Aside from issues of funding, the attitudes of the NRM and Museveni himself toward the Commission are finally exposed for what they were: a clever attempt to gain the support of those both inside Uganda and around the world who would be impressed by its appointment. This is nowhere more clear than in the funding of the new Uganda Human Rights Commission by international aid agencies and governments, contrasted with Museveni's willingness to sacrifice human rights in order to achieve his goals. Similarly, the virtual absence of the Ministry of Justice and other Ministers from the Commission, even in times of desperation, reveal the extremely low levels of support the Commission actually enjoyed.

The absence of supportive political will, combined with the institutional failures of the Commission, have resulted in the failed memory of the majority of Ugandans. I have found little evidence at all of any lasting impact of the Commission, except among the Commissioners themselves. The legacy of the Commission, in effect, has been relegated to that one dusty closet.

The International Criminal Court Has Contributed to Prospects for Peace in Uganda

Nick Grono and Adam O'Brien

In the following viewpoint, Nick Grono and Adam O'Brien, associates of an international nongovernmental organization, assert that the International Criminal Court (ICC) has played an important role in bringing about a peace initiative that has improved the security and humanitarian situation in northern Uganda. ICC investigations, they contend, encouraged and reinforced trends toward peace in Uganda and elsewhere in the region. Two reasons for this are that the threat of prosecution unnerved the military leaders of the Lord's Resistance Army (LRA) enough to bring them to the negotiating table and that the investigations made it harder for the LRA to enjoy continued support from Sudan. In addition, the investigations captured the interest of the international community, generating a broad base of regional and international support for the peace process. Grono is vice president for advocacy and operations at the International Crisis Group. O'Brien is the International Crisis Group's Uganda analyst.

For the last 20 years, the people of northern Uganda have suffered at the hands of the vicious Lord's Resistance Army (LRA), and have been penned in by the brutal response of the Ugandan government. The LRA's leaders, headed by the mystic Joseph Kony, claimed to be on a spiritual mission to cleanse northern Uganda and to rule the country according to the Ten Commandments, but have recently tried to recast themselves as freedom fighters for the politically and economically marginalised region. Regardless of their motivations, the LRA has unleashed a reign of terror primarily on the people of northern Uganda, abducting tens of thousands of children and adults, turning them into rebel soldiers, porters and sex slaves, and killing or mutilating indiscriminately.

Unfortunately, the Ugandan government's response has been little better than the problem it purports to address. The government herded over a million of the north's inhabitants (predominantly Acholi) into squalid, insecure camps—condemning them to a life removed from their fertile land, with little hope for a productive future. Every week, according to the government's own statistics, a thousand people on average die from conflict-related disease and malnutrition.

The Peace Initiative

For the first time in around a decade, a sustained peace process is taking place between the LRA and the Ugandan government. The talks are occurring in Juba, Southern Sudan, mediated by the Government of Southern Sudan. One complicating factor in the negotiations is that the ICC [International Criminal Court] is prosecuting the leadership of the LRA. The ICC has come under intense criticism in northern Uganda since the announcement in January 2004 that the Ugandan government had made the first state party referral to the ICC. The Court has been condemned by a wide range of international NGOs [nongovernmental organizations], academics, mediators and northern Ugandans. These critics argued that the threat of international prosecutions would undermine fragile local peace initiatives; would prolong the conflict by obliterating the LRA's incentive to negotiate; and would make displaced northern Ugandans even more vulnerable to LRA attacks.

In addition to criticising the timing of the ICC's investigation, some observers asserted that the Court's brand of retributive punishment was fundamentally at odds with local values, enshrined culturally in traditional reconciliation ceremonies and legally in Uganda's Amnesty Act of 2000. The ICC's intervention, opponents argued, would ultimately perpetuate rather than prevent conflict.

Some three years later, the exact opposite has happened. We are in the midst of the most promising peace initiative in the last 20 years; one that has dramatically improved the security and humanitarian situation in northern Uganda. A landmark cessation of hostilities agreement removed most LRA combatants from Uganda, allowing hundreds of thousands of war-weary civilians to begin the process of resettlement and redevelopment. The elusive and erratic LRA has tentatively begun to open up, building lines of communication with both northern Ugandans and the government. These emerging signs of trust and confidence help to promote reconciliation and to pave the way home for displaced populations. Rather than driving the LRA back into the bush, the rebels have been drawn in to negotiations. Rather than making civilians more vulnerable, northern Uganda is safer and life is slowly improving.

How did we get here? We need to be careful about placing too much credit at the feet of the ICC. An array of political and military developments in the region—most notably the signing of Sudan's CPA [Comprehensive Peace Agreement] and improved performance by the Ugandan army—have increased the costs of continued conflict for the LRA. These shifts have cut off the rebels' room for tactical and strategic manoeuvre and have compelled the LRA leadership to explore a negotiated settlement more vigorously than in the past.

Ways the ICC Investigations Helped

We would argue that the ICC's investigations played an active, positive role in encouraging and reinforcing these regional trends for the following four reasons.

First, the threat of prosecution clearly rattled the LRA military leadership, pushing them to the negotiating table. Joseph Kony and the LRA commanders are acutely aware that the ICC hangs as a sword over their heads. The issuance of arrest warrants in particular created an incentive to reach a settlement. It may be that the LRA's decision to pull most of its troops out of northern Uganda and to issue standing orders not to attack anyone in the area is in part due to deterrence by the ICC. The LRA continues to attack civilians in Southern Sudan, perhaps in the belief that it is beyond the geographic limits of the referral.

Second, the ICC's investigation made it more difficult for the LRA to enjoy continued support from its key foreign ally, Sudan. Beginning in 1994 [Sudan's capital city of] Khartoum provided an umbilical cord to Kony in the form of a steady stream of weapons, training and transportation. For Khartoum, the ICC's case increased the stakes for supporting the LRA and prompted the Government of Sudan to sign a 2005 memorandum of understanding with the Court to cooperate with arrest warrants issued against LRA commanders. Regardless of whether Khartoum actually fell within the orbit of the ICC's criminal investigation, the threat had a deterrent impact.

Some caution is necessary here. Other factors may have been more significant than the ICC in influencing Khartoum's calculations and decision to desist from supporting the LRA to the same extent as in the past. Pursuant to the CPA, for example, the Sudanese Armed Forces (SAF) pulled out of Southern Sudan, cutting off the LRA's supply lines and depriving the rebels of bases of sanctuary.

Third, the ICC's investigation raised awareness and focused the attention of the international community, which in turn provided a crucial broad base of regional and international support for the fledgling peace process. One of the key problems of previous peace initiatives was weak external support. Now, in Juba, the international community has stepped up its engagement, and

Soldiers of the Lord's Resistance Army (LRA) pose with their weapons in June 2006. The International Criminal Court has pressured the LRA to negotiate with the Ugandan government. © Sam Farmer/Getty Image News/Getty Images.

the UN [United Nations] and a number of countries are providing significant support for the talks.

Fourth, the ICC's attempt to hold the LRA leadership criminally liable for its atrocities in northern Uganda has embedded accountability and victims' interests in the structure and vocabulary of the peace process. The third point on the five point negotiating agenda is devoted to reconciliation and accountability. The parties to the talks have accepted, in principle, that robust accountability (in the form of a special chamber of the High Court and community-based rituals) is inevitable—although we should remain very sceptical of the LRA's commitment to this principle. Whether sincere or not, the LRA is being pushed towards accountability on multiple fronts by multiple actors. Consultation with the victims will play a crucial role in attempting to devise robust local accountability mechanisms. The ICC's impact is apparent insofar as this has never happened in previous initiatives with the LRA or any of the other myriad rebel groups that have emerged in Uganda since President [Yoweri] Museveni came to power in 1986.

Key Policy Considerations

While the ICC's overall contribution to the prospects for peace in Uganda has been positive, the tension between peace and justice comes into sharpest relief when the detailed provisions of a peace deal are being negotiated. Foremost among the obstacles to a Juba agreement (let alone the implementation of such a deal), is the conflict between the ICC prosecutions and the desire of the LRA's leaders for full or substantial impunity. Kony and his commanders state that they will not do a deal unless and until the ICC prosecutions are dropped. Fear of arrest means that they avoid Juba and issue instructions by satellite phone.

As the ICC Prosecutor continues to investigate participants in ongoing, or recently ended, conflicts, the international community will increasingly confront these peace and justice dilemmas. How should it balance the range of competing, and often conflicting, public policy goals in such situations? There are no clear-cut answers to these problems. Instead, we set out below some of the key considerations that policymakers should take into account when confronted with such issues.

Prosecution by the ICC is one of the few credible threats faced by leaders of warring parties

One of the main challenges for international policymakers in their efforts to resolve conflicts is that they often lack incentives or sanctions of sufficient credibility to influence the calculations of the warring parties. . . . The threat of prosecution . . . can have a salutary effect on those contemplating state-sponsored atrocities, but only if there is a real likelihood that they may face the consequences of their policies. Unfortunately, this is a stick that loses much of its deterrent power when actually applied to those still in office. Government officials who are the subject of ICC prosecution have a strong incentive to cling to power at all costs so as to avoid arrest. . . .

The ICC must secure convictions to ensure its credibility and requires strong international support to do so

The ICC needs to secure convictions to ensure its credibility as a deterrent to future perpetrators. This is going to be a challenge. In Darfur [Sudan] and Uganda the Court is going to find it extremely difficult to get hold of those it is prosecuting. And there will always be the risk of its prosecutions being trumped by peace processes.

In Uganda, the Ugandan army has failed to defeat the LRA for more than 20 years. While the Ugandan forces have recently improved their capabilities, the LRA has been able to take refuge in neighbouring countries. The lack of a coordinated response by those countries and the broader international community has ensured that the rebel group has been able to continue its attacks. It also means that the ICC cannot arrest those it wishes to prosecute. If the peace talks fail to achieve a satisfactory outcome, international efforts will have to be redoubled to arrest the indictees. . . .

Impunity should always be a last resort

The crux of the whole 'peace versus justice' debate is what should be done when a warring party (or parties) insists that a prospective peace deal is conditional on a halt to international criminal prosecutions. In these circumstances, the overriding policy issue is whether the important but uncertain prospect of deterring future perpetrators and reducing future conflicts takes precedence over more certain benefits of an immediate end to an ongoing conflict. The first point that needs to be acknowledged is that peace deals that sacrifice justice often fail to produce peace. . . .

In other contexts, however, past deals that have offered limited or full immunity from prosecution have helped bring an end to conflict and instability. . . .

The Rome Statute that governs the ICC offers ways to reach a peace deal by including robust accountability mechanisms. Such mechanisms should aim to combine traditional reconciliation ceremonies and formal legal processes in a way that satisfies both the victims' needs for justice and meets the Rome Statute's standards for accountability. . . .

Resolving Justice and Peace Goals

We also need to bear in mind that the ICC may be less of a deterrent to rebel groups than state actors, at least until the late stages of their rebellion, by which time it is too late for them to ameliorate their conduct to escape prosecution. Most rebellions fail, and most rebels embarking on their challenge to the central government are unlikely to be concerned that they may later be prosecuted for their atrocities. For these individuals, survival and success are probably much more immediate concerns. All of this means that, in the Uganda situation, the prosecution of Kony and his fellow leaders—however meritorious and warranted—may have to be justified on grounds other than its deterrent impact on potential future rebel leaders. . . .

An assessment of the ICC's impact on the Uganda conflict, and of considerations arising from other conflicts such as that in Darfur, cannot provide a straightforward answer to the question of how best to resolve competing justice and peace goals. On the one hand, ICC prosecution has, arguably, been successful where other attempts have failed in forcing Kony to the negotiating table, and providing him with incentives to explore seriously the option of a peace agreement. Yet, as the peace talks progress, it is clear that the ICC remains a very real obstacle to achieving an end to the conflict.

Much can be done to accommodate the need for peace with the demands of justice, particularly through the mechanism of Uganda's own justice system. In the end, however, difficult choices have to be made about how to balance the need for peace with the acute importance of accountability, deterrence and the strengthening of the institution of the ICC.

The International Criminal Court Is Biased

Tim Allen

In the following viewpoint, researcher Tim Allen contends that the International Criminal Court (ICC) was biased in its intervention in northern Uganda. Even though the chief prosecutor stated that the court was impartial, observers were doubtful because the court was initiated by the Ugandan president. Critics feared the ICC would punish the Lord's Resistance Army but not the government-controlled army, which committed many abuses over the years. The ICC's unwillingness to explain its role in Uganda led skeptics to believe it was hiding its true agenda. Allen is a researcher at the Crisis States Research Centre at the London School of Economics.

The impression that the ICC [International Criminal Court] intervention in Uganda is biased was given right at the start by the fact that Chief Prosecutor [Luis] Moreno-Ocampo and President [Yoweri] Museveni held a joint press briefing in January 2004, announcing that the ICC would begin preliminary investigations into 'the situation concerning the Lord's Resistance Army' [LRA]. Even human rights organisations that had lobbied strongly for the setting up of the Court expressed

Tim Allen, "War and Justice in Northern Uganda: An Assessment of the International Criminal Court's Intervention," Special Report, 2005. London, UK: Crisis States Research Centre. Copyright © 2005 by T. Allen. All rights reserved. Reproduced by permission.

concern. Amnesty International, while welcoming the announcement, chose to make the point that: "Any Court investigation of war crimes and crimes against humanity in northern Uganda must be part of a comprehensive plan to end impunity for all such crimes, regardless of which side committed them and the level of the perpetrator." Amnesty International has published numerous reports and briefings on atrocities in the region, many of which are alleged to have been perpetrated by the Ugandan security forces. So the implication was clear: the Court should also consider prosecution of people associated with the Uganda Government, something that it is empowered to do by the Rome Statute.[1] In response to this and other statements from human rights and development agencies, the Chief Prosecutor clarified his Office's position in February, and reiterated it in a formal letter to the President of the Court on 17th June 2004:

> My Office has informed the Ugandan authorities that we must interpret the scope of the referral consistently with the principles of the Rome Statute, and hence we are analysing crimes within the situation of northern Uganda by whomever committed.

Bias in Favor of the Government

However, this clarification has done little to challenge the view that the Office of the Prosecutor is acting on behalf of President Museveni, and will not attempt to punish the UPDF [Uganda People's Defense Force] as well as the LRA. There are several reasons for this. As [professor] Adam Branch points out, alleged UPDF abuses have been public knowledge for years, with no adverse effect for the Ugandan Government. On the contrary, 'essential US support for the Ugandan military has increased to include, since September 11, 2001, funds earmarked to eliminate LRA "Terrorists."' It also seems unlikely that President Museveni would have initiated the prosecution if he thought he could not control it. As noted above, he has recently suggested

Former United Nations secretary-general Kofi Annan (right) is welcomed by Ugandan president Yoweri Museveni at the opening of the Review Conference of the Rome Statute of the International Criminal Court proceedings in Kampala, Uganda, in May 2010. © AP Images/ Stephen Wandera.

that he can ask the ICC to stop proceedings if they are no longer deemed necessary. Technically he may be wrong, but it reveals his frame of mind. Even if the ICC decides that an investigation into alleged UPDF crimes is appropriate, the opposition of the Ugandan Government to such a process would make things very difficult and, given the hostility of the US to the Court, it seems improbable that there will be concerted international pressures brought to bear to make it feasible. Some legal analysts have additionally noted that serious complications could arise from an attempt to prosecute both sides, in that arguments presented by the prosecution in one case might form part of the defence in another (and vice versa).

For some commentators, the biased nature of the ICC's intervention also seems to be confirmed by rumours that the investigators' use Ugandan Government vehicles and officials to facilitate their inquiries on the ground, and by the apparent secrecy that has surrounded the ICC since mid 2004, when the formal investigation by the OTP [Office of the Prosecutor] began. The latter has given the impression that the ICC has things to hide. In addition, the paucity of information from the ICC since the initial press releases about the referral has meant that the wording of those documents has been given great weight— perhaps more than was intended. They are still the first things that come up about Uganda on the ICC website, and the Chief Prosecutor's subsequent clarification is often ignored (or dismissed).

There have been no significant efforts by the ICC Registry to counter these perceptions or promote awareness and understanding of what the Court is supposed to be doing in Uganda. As a result, most of those who have tried to follow events closely are sceptical about Chief Prosecutor Moreno-Ocampo's claims to objectivity, and anticipate that warrants will only be issued for [LRA leader Joseph] Kony and a handful of his top commanders. While there is widespread acceptance that these people are responsible for appalling acts, several commentators take the view that to focus on them alone cannot lead to a just outcome.

Expressions of Doubt About ICC Objectivity

Here are a few quotes illustrating this concern about objectivity. The first is from Barney Afako of Justice Resources. He is one of the leading legal analysts of the ICC investigation. . . .

> The Prosecutor has to prioritise. . . . His prioritisation is to go after a few people, but only those who are most responsible. . . . Also I suspect that he will . . . go for the most serious crimes. I would be surprised if he sought to prosecute more than about five people. . . . The UPDF is unlikely to be prosecuted . . . because of the difficulty of making the charges stick. . . .

The second quote is from an interview with the outspoken retired Bishop Mcleod Ochola, vice president of ARLPI [Acholi

Religious Leaders Peace Initiative], interviewed in English in November 2004.

> The ICC will not be a solution. We want the whole story to be told. . . . If they just investigate the LRA, it will be an injustice to society. . . . The ICC cannot impose itself on people. The government is inviting it, so it has already lost its impartiality. It is an injustice. . . . We have not invited it. They are already biased. It is an abuse. . . . The ICC is just full of corruption. . . . The government has killed. They have all killed. The LRA has done bad things, so has the government. We need to investigate everything. . . . The ICC is an enticement for individuals to oppose individuals. . . .

A next quote comes from Onan Acana, the Paramount Chief Elect (he was crowned on January 17th 2005). It is taken from an interview in English also in November 2004.

> How can the ICC be impartial if it is only working on one side of the conflict? There should be justice, administered impartially. . . . We have had soldiers raping men. We have had people thrown in pits. . . . Where government soldiers have committed crimes, should we just ignore it? The ICC says that if the government atrocities are as bad as LRA atrocities they will investigate. I will wait and see. . . .

Most of those we interviewed in the displacement camps did not know enough about the ICC to comment on the issue. However, several noted that the Uganda Government forces should also be investigated. For example, one Local Council officer told us that, "There are also notorious commanders on the government side. They also committed inhumane acts. . . ."; and a former LRA combatant remarked that, "The current Government was also abducting people to fight for them during the previous war. Why can't the ICC allow the community to give testimonies, because some people were abducted by the Government to become soldiers?"

Given the unwillingness of the ICC to explain what it is doing it is hard to refute the claim that it will be biased. . . .

Note

1. The Rome Statute is the treaty that established the ICC and gives it jurisdiction over three main classes of offenses: genocide, crimes against humanity, and war crimes.

CHAPTER 3

Personal Narratives

Chapter Exercises

1. **Writing Prompt**

   Imagine you are a Christian minister or Asian noncitizen living and working in Uganda during the rule of Idi Amin. Write a one-page journal entry describing your feelings about the persecution you and others are experiencing.

2. **Group Activity**

   Form groups and develop five interview questions that could be used in conducting oral histories of young Indian Ugandans exiled from their own country during the brutal regime of Idi Amin, family members who were separated during the exile, or villagers housing exiled Ugandans.

A Christian Ugandan Is Persecuted

F.K. Sempangi

In the following viewpoint, F.K. Sempangi, a Christian Ugandan, describes his experience as an evangelical living in Uganda in the early 1970s when Christians were being persecuted. He relates how upon their return to Uganda after studying and working overseas, he and his wife began Bible classes in their home and helped initiate radio and television programs. The house group grew into a church, and he describes the series of events that forced him and his wife to go into hiding and then flee Uganda entirely. At the time this viewpoint was written, Sempangi was living in exile in the United States and studying theology at Westminster Theological Seminary. He went on to author A Distant Grief: The Real Story Behind the Martyrdom of Christians in Uganda, *become a member of Parliament in the Ugandan government, and found the Presbyterian Church in Kampala.*

In the reprisals following Idi Amin's 1971 coup in Uganda, the mayor of Masaka, a town in West Buganda, was dragged from his house by Nubians [Ugandans of Sudanese descent] paid by the General. A crowd gathered. The mayor asked to speak to the

F.K. Sempangi, "Uganda's Reign of Terror," *Worldview*, vol. 18, no. 5, May 1975, pp. 16–18.

new chief of state by telephone. Amin's killers—"soldiers" is too good a word for them—stripped him, bound his hands, and tied a rope around his neck. The chief killer drew a knife, cut off the mayor's penis, and, holding it in front of the screaming man, told him he could call [the capital city of] Kampala through the severed organ.

Onlookers were dumbfounded, relatives wept; the Nubians laughed.

Mutilation and death by political assassination were common throughout Uganda in 1971, the year I returned there with my family from graduate study in Europe. . . .

Back in Uganda: New Beginnings

In June, 1971, we were back in Uganda with high professional hopes and a passionate desire to proclaim Christ. I had a teaching job at the School of Fine Art, Makerere University, my alma mater in Kampala. My wife Penina started as a nursing sister at Mulango, the country's largest hospital. Penina qualified as a midwife nurse in London while I was studying at the Royal College of Art. For a year before leaving Europe we lived in Holland, where I began a doctoral program in art history with Professor H.R. Rookmaaker at the Free University in Amsterdam.

Five months after our homecoming we opened Bible classes in our house. With some students we launched radio and television programs, and soon the house group grew into a church. We moved to a YMCA [Young Men's Christian Association] building and eventually into the open. Our community of twenty became a congregation of four thousand.

Growth in Spite of Persecution

Then all Christian programs were banned from the air waves. A native pastor was accused of treason and then killed for reading on a regular church broadcast an Old Testament prophecy of Israel's future triumph over its enemies. He was charged with supporting the modern Jewish cause.

Churchgoers leave Sunday worship service in southwest Uganda. Many Ugandan Christians were persecuted for their religious activities during Idi Amin's rule. © Nigel Pavitt/AWL Images/Getty Images.

Although denied access to mass media, our church continued to grow—from four thousand to twelve thousand. People from all walks of life turned to the Lord. Five secret police spies sent to monitor my sermons were converted.

One aim of our church was to encourage young people of talent to go abroad for ministerial training. I had an opportunity to discuss this interest with Professor Rookmaaker and officials of the L'Abri Fellowship in April, 1975, when I went to Holland, taking my family, to present papers for my doctoral finals. L'Abri, the Swiss-based evangelical organization, agreed to sponsor three of our young people in its Bible orientation course.

The Need to Hide

Despite the misgivings of friends and a warning that I should travel incognito, we returned to Uganda in September. We were intercepted at Entebbe Airport by those who loved us, and taken into hiding. Church elders came in the night to brief me on recent events. Amin's Nubians had decided to arrest and kill me. Two days earlier the secret police had gone to church headquarters, fired their weapons, molested people, and made arbitrary arrests. They were furious when I was not among those seized. Our people were released after interrogation.

Our house was invaded the very day of our return. I learned also that three weeks previously Amin's forces had set out to murder the Reverend Adoniya Kirinda, the man I left in charge of the church in my absence. The Nubians found a new convert in Kirinda's house and, because the man was well dressed, mistook him for the minister. They shot the convert eight times, dragged the body outside, and drove over it with a jeep. Panic-stricken, Kirinda went into hiding. He lived in the bush until through God's providence, he escaped to America.

The departure of Kirinda left our orphanage with no director. The facility was run with the help of Stitchting Redt Een Kind, a Dutch organization in which Mrs. Rookmaaker, wife of the professor, is active. Just as Mrs. Rookmaaker's work has saved the lives of many children, it was her foresight that spared us in September, 1973. Our friend was convinced we should not stay in Uganda. With the assistance of the Bureau for Foreign Students at Frije, the Free University, she obtained emergency airline tickets for us. Those tickets were vital in our escape.

Escape from Uganda

Two days in Uganda and a report came that our hiding place was known to the police. We had about fifteen minutes to plan an escape. The chain of events in our leaving can only be attributed to God. Since we had tickets if we could get to an airport outside Uganda, we traveled by bus toward the Kenya border. It was a risk. Could we get past the Ugandan border patrol? I felt gloomy. Near midnight we approached the checkpoint. The guards were drunk.

I stepped out of the bus as an officer walked up. He asked if I had any money. Without thinking, I took out all I had. God used my ignorance to save me from the gun. No one is supposed to cross the border with more than 150 shillings in currency. I had more than 800.

"You have too much," the guard said. "Now begin counting it into my hand."

While I counted he watched to make sure his fellow officers were not aware of the transaction. He told me to board the bus, and in five minutes we were crossing into Kenya. We flew to Holland, where I made arrangements to come to Westminster Seminary in the United States.

An Exile Recalls Incidents of Flight and Terror in Idi Amin's Uganda

Arthur Mwenkanya Katabalwa

In the following viewpoint, Arthur Mwenkanya Katabalwa, a Ugandan living in exile, describes the plight of Indian Ugandans and others under the brutal regime of Idi Amin. He describes what happened to an Indian friend and his family expelled from Uganda in 1972 by edict of Amin. He tells how they were forced to leave behind all their property and belongings and had to endure harassment and indignities while trying to leave the country. Katabalwa also shares his own experiences—what it was like as a boy to experience war firsthand and what he and his family had to do to stay alive, including fleeing from their home. He relates the surprise and delight he felt when his father, who he thought was dead, suddenly appeared to take his family home again. Katabalwa is a contributor to UNAA Times Online.

April 11th is an infamous day in the history of Uganda. Thirty years ago [1979], one of the most brutal dictators of modern times, Idi Amin, was overthrown by the armed forces of Tanzania. The events of this day have slowly been erased from the memories of many Ugandans as years after Amin was de-

Arthur Mwenkanya Katabalwa, "Memories of Idi Amin, by Amin, a Ugandan Asian in Exile," *UNAA Times Online*, April 10, 2009. Copyright 2009 by Arthur Mwenkanya Katabalwa. All rights reserved. Reproduced by permission.

posed, Uganda was still gripped in the middle of more armed conflict.

His regime was characterised by mass murder and the disappearance of many people whom he thought were his enemies. However, here in the UK [United Kingdom], one of the most poignant memories of his regime was the expulsion of Ugandan Indians in 1972. On August 4, Idi Amin ordered the expulsion of nearly 70000 Indians after an alleged dream. His accusation was that the Indians were hoarding wealth to the detriment of the local population. He ordered them to leave the country within 90 days. The resulting mayhem, as generations after generations of Indians started to plan their exit from the country, has lingered on to this day.

An Indian Family's Expulsion from Uganda

A friend of mine, Amin Parmar, who is Ugandan Indian but now lives in the UK, was only 13 when his parents told him that he was to be evacuated to the United Kingdom. Amin had grown up in the rural setting of Kassanda, a village near the capital Kampala, in all intents a small Ugandan boy. His dad was a local business man who had come to Uganda earlier and also had interests in agriculture. "My father never discussed anything at all when the trouble began," he told me. "All we were told was that we had to leave straight away".

The Parmar family had to leave the country with only the clothes they had on their backs. His father had over the years built a business empire with large swathes of land covered with sugar cane. They had factories making all sorts of produce for the local economy and many people were working for his family. But on the day that they left, they just walked out of the door and that was it. The factory keys were handed to the locals and the lorries [trucks] were given away.

On the way to the airport, the family was still harassed by the army. "My father was arrested and taken to a police station in Mityana town. We then had a few hours of anxiety as we did not know what was going to happen. The situation was very tense and we were very worried as there had been reports of some Indian women being raped and others being killed."

Departing from Uganda into Exile

"Later, an army officer that my father had known for a while arrived and managed to get him out of the police cells. We were told nothing as to why he had been held. And neither did my father talk about that episode. We were then left to proceed to the airport."

All Indians who were departing the country for countries like the UK, Canada and the USA were taken to the beach near the airport and strip searched for any gold, jewellery and other valuables. After that they were then allowed to board planes to whichever destination they were going to.

"When we arrived in the UK, we were taken to some camps in Lincolnshire where my family stayed for about nine months. We were then able to move to Stoke On Trent where we have lived ever since. Other Indians settled mainly in Leicester."

Amin Parmar still calls himself Ugandan. And I, as a Ugandan who only moved to the UK recently, was surprised at the way he spoke the local languages without any accent. He still misses the country and hopes to go back and visit one day to hopefully see some of his old friends.

A Boy on the Run in Uganda

His story really made me realise that [Idi] Amin's brutality was really shocking. Because years later, after so much suffering, I was also on the run in my own country trying to stay alive. But the good thing was that this time we had a foreign force in the country that was coming to our rescue. Amin Parmar never had that comfort. One morning as the advancing Tanzanian forces started making their presence known by the falling shells, my mother decided to take me and my two brothers to a nearby house. We lived on a boarding school campus and one of the boys' dormitories, Nigeria House, had taken a direct hit. With the dust and acrid smoke still hanging in the air, my father decided to go and collect our goats from the pastures. We did not wait for him to return. Neither did we have any belongings on us as we thought that we would be gone for a few minutes.

We only stayed at the house minutes when a shell landed yards from us and failed to explode. We scattered, heading for the surrounding villages. It was utter mayhem as several people had now been hurt by the falling shells. One of the men whom we knew well had shrapnel in his legs. We then started a 30 mile walk over three days to link up with my sister, who was in another boarding school. My mother at this time thought [it] better to unite the rest of the family and die together. She thought that my father was dead as we were getting reports that our homes were being shelled repeatedly. We were seeing war first hand. The destruction and death was everywhere.

The noise of war was deafening. And the terror on peoples' faces is something that I will never forget. My mother has only told me recently that as she struggled carrying me, she lost me for a moment and looked back only to see me on my knees praying. I cannot remember what I prayed but she hoped that my prayers would see us through. My father was meanwhile frantically looking for us through the fog of war. He decided to stay at home and look after our property.

A Return Home

Two weeks later, I was playing at a friend's house where we had taken refuge when I saw my father's Colt car. I will always remember that moment. I knew the number plate well. UYN 363. I looked through the wire mesh fence and I could see it coming up the dirt road. We were going home!! The previous night there had been a lot of bombing and we had hardly slept. Worse still we had been told that the school where we had left my father had been flattened by a seven hour battle and no one was expected to be alive. But here he was in flesh at the wheel of our old car. . . .

I was lucky that I was able to go back home and thereafter had a rather peaceful childhood in spite of the civil strife that was to follow after [Idi Amin's] fall. Amin Parmar has for the past 37 years wished and waited to go back to Uganda. He tells his children of this tiny country that he left in terror but still calls his own. Many Indians have managed to go back to Uganda and settle. But where as I got my UYN 363 moment, when my father came to pick us up, Amin Parmar has started to realise that that moment may never come for him.

A Child Soldier Escapes to Uganda

Faith J.H. McDonnell and Grace Akallo

In the following viewpoint, Grace Akallo, forced to be a soldier in the Lord's Resistance Army (LRA), shares her emotions as she tried to escape the LRA in Sudan and return to Uganda. She explains how faith and prayer gave her strength and helped keep her alive. She describes her chance encounter with a group of children, nine of whom trusted her to take them to Uganda. She goes on to describe how they summoned the courage to continue on their journey, dehydrated and close to starvation. Faith J.H. McDonnell is a writer and activist whose special interest is the future of the Acholi people of northern Uganda.

The bushes were quiet. Only the wind was blowing through the dry, scorched grass and trees, trying to shake the dead leaves. I thought Sudan was a grave for every living thing. It was the dry season, and even trees had no life in them. Nature had deprived them of water and food, and some were destroyed by fires.

I lived with these trees for three days as I walked under them. I was looking for something to eat. The dead trees could provide only a little shade with their dry branches. I would sit under them as if waiting to be dried like them. I was already dry anyway; little blood flowed in my veins. *After a few days I will be dried up like the trees,* I thought. I ate soil and leaves of trees that were still struggling to survive. I was hoping to get help from Mother Nature. That is what kept me alive for three days. But it was clear that I was going to die despite escaping all of the death around me. . . .

Children in the Wilderness

"Who are you?" a voice whispered in front of me. I aimed my AK-47 machine gun in the direction the voice came from. I was ready to defend myself.

"I am Grace," I answered. "I am from the home of teacher Lakati," I added. That is what we called the man I was given to as a wife. He had been sent back to Uganda when the camp was attacked. If he had been in the camp, he would have made things very difficult for me.

"Come on over here. Stop pointing your gun at us," the voice said.

"Okay," I answered, but I was still on my guard. [Lord's Resistance Army leader Joseph] Kony had threatened us before that the Holy Spirit would block our way if we tried to escape. Slowly I walked forward. I saw a group of children. Their eyes were misty, yet no tears fell. *We are all walking corpses,* I thought, *condemned to die in this wilderness.*

"Where are you going?" one boy from the group asked me.

"To Uganda," I answered him. But the answer was like a bitter pill in my mouth.

"Are you trying to escape?" one girl asked with suspicion in her voice.

Escape? The way it was said made me think that these children were not trying to run away. I must be careful.

Left Alone Again

"No," I lied. "I saw people go to Uganda." Really I had not seen any of us going toward Uganda. Many fled toward Juba [a city in

Southern Sudan] but I hoped to convince these children to go with me.

My lie did not work, and one boy pointed his AK-47 at me. "I am going to shoot you," he bawled at me.

"No, you are not," I said to him with a stronger voice than I had known I was capable of. "I have survived from death three times. I survived being beaten to death, I was buried alive and a bullet hit my cooking pans, yet my body was not touched. Who do you think you are to shoot me?" I added, "Go ahead and shoot me. Then I will rest from this suffering."

"Don't bother, she is going to die before reaching Uganda," another boy said. "This is one of the Aboke [a town in Northern Uganda] girls who brought this on us all. Let us leave her here."

Slowly the group of about fifty children walked away from me, their skin slack on their bones. I let them go. I was thinking that they were right. I was going to die here before someone rescued me. I did not know how many days I could survive in this dry land without food or water. I prayed for God to help me. Prayers had become my food and water. It was like I was a scapegoat. I could easily run and hide when I was threatened beyond my control.

Girls Come Back, One by One

As I was deep in my thoughts, wondering whether I was going to survive, one girl from the group came back as if to make sure I had not disappeared. "Are you sure you want to die here?" she asked as she sat near me.

"No," I replied with confidence. "I am going to Uganda."

"Do you know the way?" she asked.

"No, but God will lead me," I told her.

"It seems you know the way. I am going with you," she said.

I looked at the girl, trying to see if she was tricking me into saying that I was escaping. But the girl's eyes were true to her words. She was ready to go with me, even though I did not know the way. "If you are ready, it is okay with me," I answered her.

We quietly sat there together. The deep fears that threatened our very lives were manifested only in our eyes and the way we breathed. *Do you think you will reach Uganda?* A voice within me began tormenting me again. The voice was so loud in my ears and heart, making me lose hope.

We were both startled by the sound of the dry grass breaking. Another girl had come back. Now she sat quietly, as if waiting for some help from me or even a word. I was so tired that I just looked at her quietly with a sigh. I could have started walking away from that place, but something held me down. It was beyond hunger and thirst.

One by one the girls came back and sat near me without a word, as if the spirits would be awakened if anyone spoke. Nine girls came back to me, all expecting some help. None of us knew where it would come from. We were surrounded by evil spirits; spirits of fear had built a home in each of our hearts. We sat for a while looking from one person to another, waiting for someone to speak.

The Trek Begins

I broke the silence. "What happened? I thought you were going to Juba."

"We thought you knew the way," one girl whose name was Agnes answered me. "We want to go with you," she added.

Without stopping to think, I said, "Let's go." I got up and we started our trek, with our AK-47s strapped to our backs. We walked in silence, falling often because we were all so weak. None of us had eaten for a long time; our eyes had gone deep into our bones. We were no long human beings but dying animals. After walking for a long time, I sat down without a word to my friends. I thought I was going to pass away. I could not speak. My friends without question obeyed the silent order, and all dropped down, some on their stomachs. We were near death.

After a while, I found some strength and managed to tell my friends to sit up to pray. "Can we pray, please?" I asked. It was the first thing I had said since we started our trekking. The girls looked at me strangely but obeyed silently.

"O God, we have no strength. We are thirsty and hungry," I prayed. "Help us out of this hard land, and we will be living examples of Your love. Please help us. Amen."

The girls echoed, "Amen."

Water—Miracle and Dilemma

After our prayers, it started drizzling. At least some water was dropping from the sky, cooling down the heat that tortured our dry skin. There was a little hope. I felt like we were going to survive. We started walking again, parting the dry grass from our way and trying to put the stalks back to close our trail in case we were being followed. We reached a tributary of the Blue Nile from Sudan. First we were excited because a miracle had happened: We had water. But my heart sank when I realized that none of us could swim. I felt responsible for these kids; they came back to me, thinking I knew the way and would lead them home.

"What are we going to do?" asked Susan, one of the girls who had been quiet since we started this journey.

"I don't know," I answered her.

"I don't know how to swim, and there is no rope to tie on the other side," she said.

"I know." My brain was working, calculating how we might cross the river. This was not the first river I had had to cross since my abduction. Before it was with a group, and there was always someone who knew how to swim to go tie the rope on the other side of the river. But this day we were by ourselves. Groups had crossed the Aswa and Atebi rivers with the aid of the rope. Even then children drowned. A child would slip off the rope and would be washed away like sand. There was no screaming. They were suffocated by the angry water. The rebels felt no loss. I heard them say, "Others will be captured." This was strange to me. In my village, if someone died the whole village would mourn for that person for about two weeks. With the rebels, nobody cared. Life was like waste in the bathroom.

Crossing the River

My friends started murmuring, and Agnes spoke up. "You brought us here to die. How are we going to cross this river?"

The others just nodded in response and answered, "Yes."

"You knew all along that you did not know the way, yet you still brought us," another girl interjected. Again, others nodded in agreement.

"We will strangle you before we die," Susan said.

I was not scared of threats. My mind was past fear, yet I was angry with the girls who thought they had a reason to blame me. Did they think I had planned to bring them here to die? I composed myself with strength.

"I told you I did not know the way to Uganda, but I was trusting God to lead me. You agreed to follow me, but it was not because I said I knew the way. I did not force you to come. You just followed me in silence. Now you have turned against me, just because we can't cross the river. You know what? Let us eat the sand and drink water. Maybe we can begin thinking better." We all turned to eat the soil and drink water, as if it was going to give some miracle. *This is funny*, I thought as I gobbled the soil down and drank water to push it down into my stomach. *We fear death, yet we are walking skeletons. We are trying to run from death when it is already in us.*

"What are you going to do now?" Agnes asked after drinking water to wash down the soil she had eaten.

"I don't know," I murmured, whether to her or to myself. But she heard me.

"Well, if you don't know, we are going to kill you because you are the one who brought us here," Agnes said as she moved closer.

"No, you are not going to strangle me. I am just going to jump into this water and drown," I told her. I moved backward to the river and slipped in. I thought I would drown, but with gentle hands my God lifted my feet and put them on the growing grass in the water. I slowly crossed the river. It was a miracle, but there was no time to think about that. My friends with great surprise followed my way. One by one they crossed the river.

Glossary

Acholi Ethnolinguistic group of northern Uganda and south-ernmost South Sudan.

Acholiland Northern Uganda districts of Gulu, Kitgum, and Pader.

African Charter on Human and Peoples' Rights International human rights agreement adopted in 1981 and designed to pro-mote and protect human rights and basic freedoms in Africa; also known as the Banjul Charter.

Baganda Southern Ugandan people of Bantu origin.

Banyarwanda Term used by Ugandan leader Milton Obote's government to refer to members of ethnic groups who mi-grated to Uganda and to most of the people of western and southwestern Uganda.

Bureau of State Research Ugandan state intelligence agency.

Commission of Inquiry into Violations of Human Rights (CIVHR) Commission established by Ugandan president Yoweri Museveni in 1986 to investigate "all aspects of hu-man rights abuses" committed between December 1962 and January 1986.

Front for National Salvation (FRONASA) Ugandan rebel group founded in 1972 by Yoweri Museveni that helped over-throw Idi Amin in 1979.

Inspector General of Government (IGG) Government official tasked with protecting and promoting human rights, elimi-nating and fostering the elimination of corruption and abuse of public office, and promoting and ensuring adherence to the rule of law and justice in administration.

International Criminal Court (ICC) First permanent, treaty-based, international criminal court established to help ensure that those who commit genocide, crimes against humanity, war crimes, and crimes of aggression are penalized.

Kandooya Severe form of torture in which the upper arms are tied behind the back; introduced in Uganda in the early 1980s by the National Resistance Army.

Lord's Resistance Army (LRA) Rebel group formed by self-styled prophet Joseph Kony in the 1980s and notorious for having killed, tortured, maimed, abducted, raped, and displaced hundreds of thousands of people in Uganda and other parts of Africa.

Luwero Triangle Area of northern Uganda in which several hundred thousand people were massacred during civil wars in the 1970s and 1980s.

Makindye Military police barrack near the Ugandan capital city of Kampala that served as a prison.

National Resistance Army (NRA) Rebel army formed in 1981 and headed by Yoweri Museveni; waged a guerrilla war against the government of Milton Obote; military wing of Uganda's National Resistance Movement (NRM).

National Resistance Movement (NRM) Major Ugandan political party.

National Security Agency (NASA) Ugandan secret police.

North-south divide Division that resulted from the pattern of economic and social development that favored southern Uganda at the expense of northern Uganda.

Nubian Ugandans of Sudanese descent.

Public Safety Unit (PSU) Ugandan police unit created in 1972 to deal with armed robbers.

Rome Statute Treaty adopted in 1998 that established the International Criminal Court and gave it jurisdiction over the crime of genocide, crimes against humanity, war crimes, and the crime of aggression.

Uganda Human Rights Committee Group established in 1978 by Ugandan president Idi Amin to monitor all human rights-related information in Uganda and coordinate with the United Nations Human Rights Commission.

Uganda National Liberation Army (UNLA) Military wing of the Uganda National Liberation Front.

Uganda National Liberation Front (UNLF) Political organization of former Ugandan exiles opposed to Idi Amin's rule that became a short-term post-Amin coalition government.

Uganda National Rescue Front (UNRF) Armed rebel group in Uganda's West Nile subregion.

Uganda People's Congress (UPC) Ugandan political party founded in 1960 by Milton Obote.

Uganda People's Defense Force (UPDF) The Ugandan army, previously known as the National Resistance Army (NRA).

Uganda People's Democratic Army (UPDA) Anti–Yoweri Museveni rebel group active between 1987 and 1992.

Ujamaa Kiswahli term for the Tanzanian concept of people working together to support one another; also means the need for one to give back to those who support him or her.

West Nile Subregion in northwestern Uganda.

Organizations to Contact

The editors have compiled the following list of organizations concerned with the issues debated in this book. The descriptions are derived from materials provided by the organizations. All have publications or information available for interested readers. The list was compiled on the date of publication of the present volume; the information provided here may change. Be aware that many organizations take several weeks or longer to respond to inquiries, so allow as much time as possible.

Amnesty International
1 Easton Street
London, WC1X 0DW, United Kingdom
44-20-74135500 • fax: 44-20-79561157
website: www.amnesty.org

Amnesty International is a global movement dedicated to promoting human rights and fighting injustice. The world's largest grassroots human rights organization, with offices in more than eighty countries, it investigates and exposes abuses worldwide and educates and mobilizes the public. Its publications include *Wire*, a bimonthly magazine; e-newsletters; thematic and country reports; and annual reports on the state of the world's human rights. Its website includes a searchable library, links to human rights news by region, and a "Learn About Human Rights" section searchable by country, topic, and campaign.

Foundation for Human Rights Initiative (FHRI)
Human Rights House, Plot 1853, Lulume Road Nsambya
PO Box 11027
Kampala, Uganda
256-414-510263, 510498, 510276, 0312-266025
fax: 256-414-510498

e-mail: hri@dmail.ug
website: www.fhri.or.ug

The FHRI is a human rights advocacy organization that seeks to remove impediments to democratic development. Its mission is to enhance knowledge, respect and observance of human rights, and to promote the exchange of information and best practices through training, education, research, advocacy and strategic partnerships. Its publications include *The Defender* magazine, thematic reports such as "The Right to Health Care in Uganda," and reports such as "The National Human Rights Perception Survey," and the "Community Based Human Rights Guide."

Human Rights First
333 Seventh Avenue, 13th Floor
New York, NY 10001-5108
(212) 845-5200 • fax: (212) 845-5299
e-mail: feedback@humanrightsfirst.org
website: www.humanrightsfirst.org

Human Rights First is a New York and Washington, D.C.–based international human rights organization that seeks to promote laws and policies that advance universal rights and freedoms. It works to combat hate crimes, provide a lifeline for international human rights activists, and safeguard refugee rights. It advocates fair legal policies that respond to national security concerns and opposes US counterterrorism measures amounting to torture or unlawful detention. Its publications include strategy papers; reports such as "Disrupting the Supply Chain for Mass Atrocities: How to Stop Third-Party Enablers of Genocide and Other Crimes Against Humanity"; and "Rights Wire," a monthly e-newsletter that offers analysis of human rights issues. Its website provides links to human-rights-related blogs, news articles, and videos.

Human Rights Focus (HURIFO)
Plot 5/7 Airfield Road

PO BOX 970
Gulu-Uganda
(256) 471 432259 • fax: (256) 471 432402
e-mail: hurifo@hurifo.org
website: www.hurifo.org

HURIFO is a Ugandan nonpartisan human rights organization dedicated to protecting, improving, and promoting human
rights in Uganda and worldwide. Its publications include the
quarterly magazine *The Examiner* and research reports such as
"Fostering the Transition in Acholiland: From War to Peace and
from Camps to Home."

Human Rights Watch
Fifth Avenue, 34th Floor
New York, NY 10118-3299
(212) 290-4700 • fax: (212) 736-1300
website: www.hrw.org

Human Rights Watch is an independent international nongovernmental organization dedicated to defending and protecting
the human rights of people around the world. Its researchers
conduct investigations on human rights abuses in all regions of
the world. It challenges governments and those in power to end
abusive practices and respect international human rights law,
and it enlists the public and the international community to support the cause of human rights for all. Its publications include
newsletters and reports such as "Abducted and Abused: Renewed
War in Northern Uganda." Its website includes links to news articles and press releases, commentary, and letters, as well as videos, slideshows, photo essays, podcasts, and more.

International Crisis Group
420 Lexington Ave., Suite 2640
New York, NY 10170
(212) 813-0820 • fax: (212) 813-0825
e-mail: newyork@crisisgroup.org

website: www.crisisgroup.org

International Crisis Group is a Belgium-based nongovernmental organization committed to preventing and resolving deadly conflict. It is recognized as a leading independent, nonpartisan source of analysis and advice to governments and intergovernmental bodies on the prevention and resolution of deadly conflict. Its publications include "CrisisWatch," a bulletin that assesses on a monthly basis the current state of play in approximately seventy countries or areas of actual or potential conflict, and more than eighty reports and briefing papers annually.

Montreal Institute for Genocide and Human Rights Studies (MIGS)
Concordia University
1455 De Maisonneuve Boulevard West
Montreal, Quebec, H3G 1M8 Canada
(514) 848-2424 ext. 5729 or 2404
fax: (514) 848-4538
website: http://migs.concordia.ca

MIGS, founded in 1986, monitors native-language media for early warning signs of genocide in countries deemed to be at risk of mass atrocities. The institute houses the Will to Intervene (W2I) Project, a research initiative focused on the prevention of genocide and other mass atrocity crimes. The institute also collects and disseminates research on the historical origins of mass killings and provides comprehensive links to this and other research material on its website. The institute also provides numerous links to other websites focused on genocide and related issues, as well as specialized sites organized by nation, region, or case.

Office of the United Nations High Commissioner for Human Rights (OHCHR)
Palais Wilson, 52 rue des Pâquis, CH-1201
Geneva, Switzerland

41 22 917 9220
e-mail: InfoDesk@ohchr.org
website: www.ohchr.org

The OHCHR works for the protection of human rights for all people, helps empower people to realize their rights, and assists those responsible for upholding such rights. It supports the work of the United Nations human rights mechanisms, such as the Human Rights Council, and works to ensure the enforcement of universally recognized human rights norms. Its publications include numerous brochures, handbooks, booklets, fact sheets, reference materials, training and educational materials, and special issue papers. Its website provides links to news articles, press releases, videos, speeches, and op-eds.

STAND/United to End Genocide
1025 Connecticut Ave., Suite 310
Washington, DC 20036
(202) 556-2100
e-mail: info@standnow.org
website: www.standnow.org

STAND is the student-led division of United to End Genocide (formerly Genocide Intervention Network). STAND envisions a world in which the global community is willing and able to protect civilians from genocide and mass atrocities. In order to empower individuals and communities with the tools to prevent and stop genocide, STAND recommends activities from engaging government representatives to hosting fund-raisers, and has more than one thousand student chapters at colleges and high schools. While maintaining many documents online regarding genocide, STAND provides a plan to promote action as well as education.

United Human Rights Council (UHRC)
104 N. Belmont Street, Suite 313
Glendale, CA 91206

(818) 507-1933 • fax: (818) 240-3442
e-mail: contact@uhrc.org
website: www.unitedhumanrights.org

The UHRC works on a grassroots level toward exposing and correcting human rights violations of governments worldwide. It advances its goals and raises global awareness through grassroots mobilization, boycotts, community outreach, and education. Its publications include reports such as "The Genocide in Rwanda" and "The Darfur Genocide." Its website includes links to posts, photos, and videos.

List of Primary Source Documents

The editors have compiled the following list of documents that either broadly address genocide and persecution or more narrowly focus on the topic of this volume. The full text of these documents is available from multiple sources in print and online.

African Charter on Human and Peoples' Rights, 1981

This charter is a declaration of human rights produced by the Organization of African Unity (OAU). Meant to encourage and protect human rights and basic freedoms on the African continent, it promotes and provides for a human rights commission and establishes the concept of "peoples" rights, as well as civil, political, economic, social, and cultural rights.

The Anguish of Northern Uganda: Results of a Field-Based Assessment of the Civil Conflicts in Northern Uganda, 1997

This report commissioned by the United States Agency for International Development's (USAID) Office of US Foreign Disaster Assistance (OFDA) addresses the causes, progress, prognosis, economic impact, and population displacement dimensions of conflicts in the north-central Ugandan districts of Gulu and Kitgum and the West Nile districts of Arua, Moyo, and Nebbi.

Convention Against Torture and Other Cruel, Inhuman, or Degrading Punishment, United Nations, 1974

This draft resolution adopted by the United Nations General Assembly in 1974 opposes any nation's use of torture, unusually harsh punishment, and unfair imprisonment.

Convention on the Prevention and Punishment of the Crime of Genocide, 1948

This resolution of the United Nations General Assembly defines genocide in legal terms and advises participating countries to prevent and punish actions of genocide in war and peacetime.

Country Report of the Research Project by the International Labour Organization and the African Commission on Human and Peoples' Rights on the Constitutional and Legislative Protection of the Rights of Indigenous Peoples: Uganda, 2009

This report addresses the status and trends relative to the constitutional, legislative, and administrative protection of the rights of indigenous peoples in Uganda. It includes recommendations for government actions to more fully address the concerns of indigenous peoples.

Human Rights Report: Uganda, 2010

This report issued by the US Department of State addresses the prevailing status of human rights in Uganda and identifies specific incidents within seven different human-rights-related categories, including respect for the integrity of the person, respect for civil liberties, and respect for political rights.

Miscellaneous Cause No. 163 of 2010

This court ruling addresses a court case and verdict in a 2010 suit brought against a Ugandan newspaper, which published an anti-gay article that allegedly threatened the rights of the individuals bringing the suit.

Principles of International Law Recognized in the Charter of the Nuremburg Tribunal, United Nations International Law Commission, 1950

After World War II (1939–1945) the victorious allies legally tried surviving leaders of Nazi Germany in the German city of Nuremburg. The proceedings established standards for international law that were affirmed by the United Nations and by later court tests. Among other standards, national leaders can be held responsible for crimes against humanity, which might include "murder, extermination, deportation, enslavement, and other inhuman acts."

The Report of the Commission of Inquiry into Violations of Human Rights Committed Against Ugandans Since 1962–1968: Findings, Conclusions and Recommendations, 1994

This report addresses the results of the Inquiry Commission, and it provides a record of evidence and exhibits the commission received from witnesses.

Rome Statute of the International Criminal Court, 1998

This statute addresses the creation of the International Criminal Court and its jurisdiction over the crime of genocide, crimes against humanity, war crimes, and the crime of aggression in situations where states cannot or will not do so themselves.

Uganda: Legal Notice Creating the Commission of Inquiry into Violations of Human Rights, The Commissions of Inquiry Act, Legal Notice No. 5, 1986

This legal notice addresses the appointment of commissioners tasked with conducting inquiries into violations of human rights, breaches of the rule of law, and abuses of power committed under Ugandan governments in power from October 9, 1962, to January 25, 1986, and recommending possible ways of preventing such violations from happening in the future. It identifies specific areas of inquiry and gives the commission the right to call for witnesses, request that evidence be provided, and seek help from others.

United Nations General Assembly Resolution 96 on the Crime of Genocide, 1946

This 1946 resolution defines genocide, affirms that genocide is a crime under international law, and asks that legislation be enacted to prevent and punish said crime.

Universal Declaration of Human Rights, United Nations, 1948

This declaration, the first set of human rights principles to apply to all the nations of the world, addresses the civil, political, economic, social, and cultural rights to which all people worldwide are entitled, no matter their nationality, race, or gender.

Whitaker Report on Genocide, 1985

This report addresses the question of the prevention and punishment of the crime of genocide. It calls for the establishment of an international criminal court and a system of universal jurisdiction to ensure that genocide is punished.

For Further Research

Books

Tim Allen and Koen Vlassenroot (eds.), *The Lord's Resistance Army: Myth and Reality*. London: Zed Books, 2010.

Jaffar Amin and Margaret Akulia, *Idi Amin: Hero or Villain?: His Son Jaffar and Other People Speak Out*. Vancouver, British Columbia, Canada: Millennium Global, 2010.

Omongole R. Anguria, *Apollo Milton Obote: What Others Say*. Oxford, England: African Books Collective Limited, 2006.

Tony Avirgan and Martha Honey, *War in Uganda: The Legacy of Idi Amin*. Westport, CT: Lawrence Hill and Company, 1982.

Adam Branch, *Displacing Human Rights: War and Intervention in Northern Uganda*. Oxford, England: Oxford University Press, 2011.

Kathy Cook, *Stolen Angels: The Kidnapped Girls of Uganda*. New York: Penguin, 2009.

Chris Dolan, *Social Torture: The Case of Northern Uganda, 1986–2006*. Oxford, England: Berghahn Books, 2011.

Donald H. Dunson, *Child, Victim, Soldier: The Loss of Innocence in Uganda*. Maryknoll, NY: Orbis Books, 2008.

Sverker Finnström, *Living with Bad Surroundings: War, History, and Everyday Moments in Northern Uganda*. Durham, NC: Duke University Press, 2008.

Kizito Michael George, *Human Rights and Patrimonial Politics: Challenges to the Social and Legal Enforcement of Human Rights in Uganda*. Saarbrücken, Germany: VDM Verlag Dr. Mueller, 2010.

Wojciech Jagielski, *The Night Wanderers: Uganda's Children and the Lord's Resistance Army*. New York: Seven Stories Press, 2012.

A.B.K. Kasozi, *The Social Origins of Violence in Uganda, 1964–1985*. Montreal, Canada: McGill-Queen's University Press, 1995.

Wycliffe Kato, *Escape from Idi Amin's Slaughterhouse*. London; New York: Quartet Books, 1989.

Henry Kyemba, *A State of Blood*. New York: Ace Books (Penguin Group USA), 1977.

Yoweri R. Museveni, *Sowing the Mustard Seed: The Struggle for Freedom and Democracy in Uganda*. London: MacMillan, 1997.

Phares Mutibwa, *Uganda Since Independence: A Story of Unfulfilled Hopes*. Trenton, NJ: Africa World Press, 1992.

Thomas P. Ofcansky, *Uganda: Tarnished Pearl of Africa*. Boulder, CO: Westview Press, 1996.

Richard Okello, *The Massacres of Uganda: Eye Witness Accounts of the Worst Civil War in World History*. Charlotte, NC: CreateSpace, 2011.

Adam Seftel, *Uganda: The Bloodstained Pearl of Africa and Its Struggle for Peace*. Kampala, Uganda: Fountain, 1994.

George Ivan Smith, *Ghosts of Kampala: The Rise and Fall of Idi Amin*. New York: St. Martin's Press, 1980.

Periodicals and Internet Sources

Sheryl Henderson Blunt, "The Devil's Yoke," *Christianity Today*, March 2007.

Daniella L. Boston, "Genocide in Uganda: The African Nightmare Christopher Hitchens Missed," *Acholi Times*, May 17, 2006. www.acholitimes.com.

Jane Bussmann, "Joseph Kony: Uganda's Enemy Number One," *The Telegraph*, July 22, 2010. www.telegraph.co.uk.

C.J. Chivers, "'All People Are the Same to God': An Insider's Portrait of Joseph Kony," *The New York Times*, January 9, 2012. http://atwar.blogs.nytimes.com.

Elizabeth Day, "Why Was I Born Gay in Africa," *The Observer*, March 26, 2011. www.guardian.co.uk.

Christopher Hitchens, "Childhood's End," *Vanity Fair*, January 2006.

Paul Jeffrey, "Hope for Uganda: In the Wake of Violence, a Campaign for Forgiveness," *America*, August 18, 2008.

Justice and Reconciliation Project Gulu District NGO Forum, "Community Peace Building and Reconciliation: A Case Study of Peer Support in Pajule," *Field Notes,* no. 10, July 2009. http://justiceandreconciliation.com.

Ronnie Layoo and James Eriku, "ICC Calls for Patience over Kony Arrest," *Daily Monitor*, May 3, 2011. www.monitor .co.ug.

Neelima Mahajan-Bansal, "Heart of Darkness," *Forbes India Magazine*, August 14, 2009. http://forbesindia.com.

Ogenga Otunnu, "The Path to Genocide in Northern Uganda," *Refuge*, vol. 17, no. 3, August 1998. https://pi.library.yorku.ca.

Paul Raffaele, "Uganda: The Horror," *Smithsonian*, February 2005.

Abbey K. Semuwemba, "Musevani's Luwero Triangle War Was Justified," *Uganda Correspondent*, October 18, 2010. www .ugandacorrespondent.com.

Sylvia Tamale, "A Human Rights Assessment of the Ugandan Anti-homosexuality Bill 2009," *The Equal Rights Review*, vol. 4, 2009. www.equalrightstrust.org.

Wall Street Journal, "Imperiled Continent—Luckless Land: Idi Amin May be Gone, But Ruinous Violence Continues in Uganda—Murders, Disappearances Are Rife as Various Factions Fight with One Another—'Life Gets Worse and Worse,'" July 24, 1985.

Henry Wasswa, "Forced to Be Killers, Ugandan Youths Struggle for Normal Life, Rehabilitation," *Los Angeles Times*, February 22, 1998.

Emily Wax, "New Direction in Uganda's Old War; Government Arms Militia to Fight Rebels," *Washington Post*, February 16, 2004.

Rebecca Wearn, "The Long Wait for Peace," *New Internationalist*, August, 2007. www.newint.org.

Roger P. Winter, "Uganda: Creating a Refugee Crisis," *Cultural Survival Quarterly*, no. 7.2, 1983.

Roger P. Winter, "The Armies of Uganda and Human Rights—A Personal Observation," *Cultural Survival Quarterly*, no. 11.4, 1987.

Dan Wooding, "How Idi Amin, the 'Butcher of Uganda' Changed My Life—for Good," Assist News Service, March 16, 2010. www.assistnews.net.

Other

Allafrica.com/Uganda (www.allafrica.com/uganda). This website provides documents and resources; news reports and headlines from African and worldwide sources; links to featured posts and articles; and information about various topics, including human rights.

Between Two Fires: Torture and Displacement in Northern Uganda (2006). This documentary addresses the torture and displacement issues experienced by internally displaced persons in Uganda's Acholiland.

General Idi Amin Dada: A Self-Portrait (1974). This documentary addresses the life and regime of Ugandan president Idi Amin.

In a Soldier's Footsteps (2005). This documentary addresses the events that transpire when a former child soldier in the rebel army in Uganda, currently a refugee in Denmark, receives news that the missing son he thought dead is a child soldier, and he returns to Uganda to get him back.

Invisible Children (2006). This documentary addresses the plight of northern Uganda's night commuters, children who each night walk miles to places of refuge to escape being abducted and turned into child soldiers by Joseph Kony and his Lord's Resistance Army.

Invisible Children (www.invisiblechildren.com). This website provides articles, updates, video clips, and blogs about the Lord's Resistance Army (LRA), its activities and victims, and its leader, Joseph Kony. It provides a video introduction to an LRA crisis tracker, a site whose real-time mapping platform and data collection system records and tracks LRA activities and offers videos, photos, and reports of LRA activities.

The Last King of Scotland (2006). This feature film, based on factual events of Ugandan dictator Idi Amin's rule, tells the fictional story of a young Scottish doctor who travels to Uganda and becomes Amin's personal physician.

Mississippi Masala (1991). This feature film addresses the resettlement in the United States of an Indian family forced to leave Uganda in 1972 when Ugandan president Idi Amin expelled Asians from his country.

Ugandan Civil Society Coalition on Human Rights and Constitutional Law (www.ugandans4rights.org). This website provides up-to-date information on Uganda's proposed Anti-Homosexuality Bill, including the perspectives of

Ugandans opposed to the legislation. It includes an open forum on which to share views on constitutionalism in Uganda, publications about the bill, a press room, and issue-related videos.

Index